The Spirit Lives

PETER LANG
New York • Washington, D.C./Baltimore • Bern
Frankfurt am Main • Berlin • Brussels • Vienna • Oxford

David Howe Turner

The Spirit Lives

A Personal Journey
from Loss to Understanding
Through Religious Experience

PETER LANG
New York • Washington, D.C./Baltimore • Bern
Frankfurt am Main • Berlin • Brussels • Vienna • Oxford

Library of Congress Cataloging-in-Publication Data

Turner, David H.
The spirit lives: a personal journey from loss to understanding
through religious experience / David Howe Turner.
p. cm.
Includes bibliographical references.
1. Spiritual life. I. Title.
BL624 .T84   291.4'092−dc21   2001038449
ISBN 0-8204-5761-2

Die Deutsche Bibliothek-CIP-Einheitsaufnahme

Turner, David Howe:
The spirit lives: a personal journey from loss to understanding
through religious experience / David Howe Turner.
−New York; Washington, D.C./Baltimore; Bern;
Frankfurt am Main; Berlin; Brussels; Vienna; Oxford: Lang.
ISBN 0-8204-5761-2

Cover design by Lisa Dillon

The paper in this book meets the guidelines for permanence and durability
of the Committee on Production Guidelines for Book Longevity
of the Council of Library Resources.

© 2002 Peter Lang Publishing, Inc., New York

Printed in the United States of America

for everyone who has lost a child

There are more things in heaven and earth, Horatio,
Than are dreamt of in your philosophy
(Shakespeare, *Hamlet*,
Act I, Scene V)

TABLE OF CONTENTS

ILLUSTRATIONS

IN MEMORIAM:
PETER LANG 1928–2001

Peter Lang had intended to write a publisher's preface to this book but passed away in April before he was able to do so. The last time I talked to him was after an operation to remove a tumour from his stomach, and he seemed upbeat and hoping for a full recovery. He said that he wanted to read through the manuscript one more time so that he would fully understand the implications of the experiences recounted before committing his thoughts to paper. He had been connecting some of the things mentioned in the book to experiences he had while going into the operation—a kind of peace and awareness beyond the intellectual—but he couldn't quite find the words to describe it. He seemed to feel in touch with his companion Gisela who had passed away some years earlier and who rests on his estate at Lyday Close in Gloucestershire, where I had first met him (photo 38). Indeed, were it not for this meeting, it is doubtful I would have proceeded with this book at all.

It was the summer of 1998, and I had been to India to visit one of the characters in this story, Abdul Hamid Khan, but had become very ill from the heat and arrived in England weak and some 30 pounds lighter than when I had left a month earlier. Mr. Lang and I had been corresponding since the publication of my first book with Lang Publishing in 1985 (*Life Before Genesis*) and this was my first opportunity to meet him. He basically nursed me back to health on rösti over the next week while we discussed everything from his plan to establish a haven for homeless children at Lyday Close to mine to write about my spiritual experiences. This would, I thought, be academically unacceptable to many in my profession and might even be ridiculed. Mr. Lang told me not to worry about that but to just go ahead and write it, then decide what to do with it later. So I did. And here it is.

*   *   *   *

What impressed me most about Peter Lang was his genuine humanity and humility. Even in the face of the many trials and tribulations he was forced to deal with in his personal and business life—perhaps even because of them—a genuine kindness and compassion for others shone through. I know that he is now at peace with his beloved Gisela. I hope that in some small way I was able to help him on his journey as he, in a much larger way, was able to help me on mine. He was an old soul who will be missed.

PROLOGUE

Birth and death, the same moment, two different points in time. We wonder, we fear, we deny, we accept. We can no more prevent our passing out of this world than we can control our coming into it. However, we can decide to give someone else birth, and we can decide to terminate life, our own or someone else's, prematurely. This book is about the events surrounding a birth and a death—about four children I helped bring into the world, about two who remain, and two who left before their time. It's about discovering how selfish grief can be. Do loved ones depart before *their* time, or before *our* time? It's a book about journeying aimlessly in the aftermath of loss to the far reaches of the globe trying to find peace and in the process coming to experience directly what Aboriginal people in Australia had only been able to *tell* me about in my work with them over the past 30 years. It's about "seeing" and connecting to people through the openness of grief in the same deep and profound way that Aboriginal people connect "naturally" to each other.

*　　　*　　　*　　　*

I never really got to meet Bryan. I saw him briefly as he was being rushed in an incubator to the city at birth; he never returned. I remember him as being beautiful. For five years afterwards I referred to him as Colin, completely blocking out the loss. That was a mistake. What was just as bad was that no one corrected me.

I still miss Iain (photo 41) and it is fourteen years ago now since he passed away. At the age of five. I was 47. He had cancer.

At that time in my life I was living in my mind. I was, and still am, an academic working as an anthropologist at a university. My life was "figuring things out," analysing them, developing theories about them, debating in journals and books. Certainly my ideas were based on experiences, but *research* experiences, experiences of people, places, and events whom I encountered "in the field," doing my work, for a "scientific" purpose. Not that I didn't have experiences of the unusual. My work had taken me to Outback Australia to live with the Aborigines there, ties which I have maintained since 1969. However, it wasn't until 1986—17 years into that work—while living on Groote Eylandt and Bickerton Island with Iain (then 3) and the rest of my family—Ruth, Graeme (then 14, photo 40) and Michelle (then

6, photo 40)—that I began to take the indigenous experience seriously. That is, I began to see and hear something of what they saw and heard. I began to open myself up to experiences outside myself as they occurred independently of my preconceptions about experience. I was not alone in this in my profession. My colleague Jean–Guy Goulet, for one, had opened himself up to Dene Tha experience in his work among them in northern Alberta and has recounted the results in his book *Ways of Knowing* (Vancouver, University of British Columbia Press, 1998). However, my grief took me beyond the initial task of learning another people's language and ways of ordering things to abandoning *all* conventional ways of ordering experience, indigenous ways included.

Aborigines did teach that one could completely lose one's self in certain circumstances or by concentrating on musical forms or both. These musical forms were expressed in singing and playing their hollow–log musical instrument the *yiraga* or didjeridu. Some circumstances, they said, were so dramatic that they could plough through one's ordering apparatuses, strip them away, and allow other realities to impose themselves on consciousness. An event such as death (where they express their musical forms) was such a circumstance; certain phenomena of nature were another. Indeed, placing people in such circumstances was a way of teaching them about the extraordinary. This was sometimes how they attempted to teach me—by placing me in circumstances *so* heightened in intensity that even I could see what they were referring to.

"If you go down to the ocean at the place called A:nemura-mandja in the dry season in the late afternoon when the wind is blowing at its strongest and the tide is coming in, you will see waves laugh." I went and I did. Millions of waveforms all in rows, each one exactly the same as the other, seemingly frozen in space and time, each outlined in illuminated form, each with a wisp of whitecap streaming from its crest flowing toward another. It was at once an experience of variable matter moving between fixed forms and a perfectly proportioned *gestalt*. I sat there feeling happy and alive, chuckling away to myself, overwhelmed by the beauty of what I was seeing. The Greeks called it an *aesthetic*, "invisible presence in visible form . . . the divine enhancement of earthly life" (James Hillman, *The Soul's Code*, New York: Random House, 1996: 95). Antoine de

Saint–Exupéry expressed it this way in *The Little Prince* (New York: Harcourt and Brace, 1971: 93):

> "Yes," I said to the little prince. "The house, the stars, the desert—what gives them their beauty is something that is invisible! . . . What I see here is nothing but a shell. What is important is invisible."

*　　*　　*　　*

I have debated with myself for many years about whether or not I should tell this story. It might resurrect the pain of grief in those close to me at the time; it might even cause them some embarrassment. It might have the same effect on, and consequences for, me. After all, we live in a secular world where evidence of the spiritual is dismissed and even ridiculed by those not party to the experience. At best, most people are sceptical. In the end, though, I decided to take the risk and stand on my convictions. After experiencing what I did in the aftermath of Iain's death I now have no doubts whatsoever that the spirit lives beyond death and before life and that what connects us together–apart is, in a deep and profound way, something beyond even what we call love. It is this that sustains us in times of trouble and moves us to our finest moments.

Without doubt, sceptics will say that the experiences I am about to relate are a figment of the imagination conjured up by the psyche to relieve pain, ease loss, and enable one to continue on living without the disabling effects of grief—a kind of psychic security blanket if you will. I would counter with a "yes, but . . ."; the consequence of an understanding does not constitute its cause. Intense pain and grief may very well overwhelm the psyche to the extent that new avenues of "category–less" perception are opened up and one sees, hears, senses, things that are really there but closed to perception under normal "thinking" conditions. If extreme pain, why not extreme joy? An experience similar to the ones I had surrounding Iain's death occurred at my daughter's birth and that was indeed an occasion of extreme joy and happiness.

I kept a diary of the events surrounding Michelle's birth and Iain's death and the events that followed. What is written here is simply a record of what happened—without the advantage of hindsight, though I do occasionally interject a brief commentary from the perspective of where I am now, and I do draw some implications at the end of the journey. The three phases or parts of the journey are named, first and foremost, in Aboriginal terms, reflecting the importance of their teachings on my understanding. These are:

Nganyangwa, my spirit lives: the story of my own experience of my spiritual self, though this is not quite the sense I made of it at the time. Along with this experience, however, did come an intellectual understanding of very this–worldy phenomena that had been puzzling me at the time.

A:nelangwa, his spirit lives: the story of my experiences of Iain after he died and the sense I tried to make of this and of my own life. The attempt took me on a journey from my home in Canada through encounters with various world religions ranging from Christianity to Hinduism, Islam, Buddhism, and a Native North American tradition, against the background of what I had been taught by my Aboriginal mentors in Australia.

Yirralangwa, our spirits live: the story of where I finally arrived —back where I began—but with new understanding and awareness to confirm the relational nature of our deepest connection to one another and to other forms of life on this planet, a nature which we have neglected in the name of opportunism and "necessity."

ACKNOWLEDGMENTS

The love of my two remaining children, Michelle and Graeme, and my love for them sustained me to the point where I considered writing this book. It begins at a point where my marriage ends and Ruth and I go our separate ways. Still, she is so much a part of what led up to the events described here that I cannot help but think she is still a part of the events that happened subsequently. It is hard to know what to say to her after all these years except to beg her understanding.

In June and July of 1999 in Haibara Japan where my partner, Alexa Ponomareff, was teaching English as a second language, I revisited my diaries and recompiled my notes. In July and August I typed them up in Wakayama at the home of Yuji Ueno, a former student of mine now teaching at Poole Gakuin University in Osaka. It was Yuji who had introduced me to Zen Buddhism at Kokokuji Zen monastery a few years earlier. I thank Yuji and his extended family for their hospitality, Alexa for her patience and love.

I also want to thank four people who counselled me through the worst parts of the journey herein described: Fr. Richard Whalen now of St. Michael's church, Belleville, Dr. Robert Oxlade of Kingston, Dan Bajorek of Toronto and my friend Don Wiebe of Trinity College Toronto, as well as Trinity College itself. To my brother, John and his wife Shelly, I owe a special debt of thanks. Nor can I forget my friends at Sunday Morning Hockey in Perth, in particular Greg McNally, Bill Doyle, Dennis Cordick, Jim Caswell, and Peter Whitehead, nor Larry and Charlie Ostrom, Francis and Pat Mackler, Bob and Gay Pattison, Jim and Lorna Peden, Vivian and Gary Barr, Jim and Judy Walsh, Dr. Richard Moxon, and some former students of mine, Chris Trott, Guy Lanoue, Robert Adlam, Philip Smith –Eivemark, Morgan Gerrard, Jeremy Brett, Jessy Pagliaroli, and Philippe Rouja. And I would like to thank a current one, Magdalena Czyzycka, for her friendship and technical assistance.

The jacket photo of the author is by Jessy and the musical score of *Lord of the Dance* (page 185) by James Kippen.

I have also benefited considerably from dialogues with three colleagues who read an earlier draft of the manuscript: Jean–Guy Goulet of St. Paul's University in Ottawa, Bhupinder Singh, a Professor at Punjabi University in Patiala India, with whom I have corresponded for a few years now, and Doug Daniels of the University of Regina who has shared a parallel journey of his own. Michael Ignatieff, currently at the Carr Centre for Human Rights Policy at Harvard University was kind enough to allow me to reprint excerpts from his Larkin–Stuart Lectures at Trinity College Toronto in November of 1995. I am also grateful to Heidi Burns of Peter Lang publishing, my editor, and to Chris Myers and Lisa Dillon whose decision it was to proceed with the book. Chapter 7 is a revised version of part of my last book with Peter Lang Publishing, *Genesis Regained* (1999: 162–183).

*   *   *   *

The concluding chapter and the final draft of *The Spirit Lives* were written at my cottage on Dalhousie Lake near my hometown of Perth, Ontario in Canada. Perth is where my four children were born, and nearby Rideau Ferry is where two of them now rest; Perth is where my brother Roger, my father Norman and mother Maud (photo 39) are buried. Can one's connection to a place run any deeper than this?

PHOTOJOURNEY

1. Perth–on–the–Tay (as it was in my childhood)

2. 54 Drummond St. West (as it is today)

3. The Cottage on Otty Lake (as it is today)

4. The Farm in North Burgess Township (as it is today)

5. Trinity College, Toronto

6. Trinity College Chapel

7. My Tree, New Zealand

8. The Healing Trees

9. John (left) and Francis

10. Notre Dame du Calvaire

11. The Grotto

12. Solitude

13. "The Last Supper"

14. Chaumarga, Bali

15. Gamelan Rehearsal

16. Budigu Festival

17. The Healing Pool

18. Besakhi Temple

19. At Gandichock, Himachal Pradesh

20. The Young Guru at Brahmaur

21. Gujar Encampment

22. Trekking

23. Shrine at the Sach Pass

24. Kokokuji, Japan

25. Sougen (right) and Yuji

26. The Crying Dragon

27. Calligraphy Room

28. Sandscape, with Ducks

29. Shawanaga Band Office

1

30. At the Feast

31. Constructing the Sweat Lodge

32. Roger Jones (right) Presenting Eagle Feather

33. The Cottage on Dalhousie Lake

34. Galiyawa Wurramarrba

35. Nagulabena Warnungamadada (Lalara)

36. Nanggwara Warnungwadarrbalangwa (Bara)

37. Jabeni Warnungamadada (Lalara)

38. Peter Lang at Lyday Close

39. Norman and Maud at their 50th

PART I

NGANYANGWA,
MY SPIRIT LIVES

1

VIA RAIL

January 31, 1980. It was a cold, crisp, winter day in Toronto, the kind that reminded you of the prairies. Prairie cold is a bracing cold, one that invigorates rather than drains. Most Toronto winter days drain: overcast skies, slush instead of snow, people scurrying about outdoors on their way to being indoors. Public works crews out in a flash to clear away any traces of real winter. Toronto: the city unable to make up its mind whether it is Canadian or American. Today, however, there was no ambiguity. It was a northern place.

Well Being

Nothing, not even a Toronto winter, could dampen my spirits this day. Michelle had been born in Perth (photo 1) on Tuesday and I had come back to Toronto to teach my classes at the university. It was now Friday and I was on my way home.

I picked up my sandwich in the kitchen at Trinity College (photo 5) and headed past the Porter's Lodge and out on to Hoskin Avenue. The Museum subway station was just around the corner on Queen's Park Circle north of the Ontario legislature.

From the museum I was headed south to Union Station then east on VIA rail to Kingston and from there on to Brockville and north to Smiths Falls, where my father was going to pick me up and drive me the 12 miles (19k.) to Perth.

Down the steps I went into the subway station. Through the turnstiles, past the ticket–taker, down the escalator and on to the platform. It was about 5 p.m. Graeme was seven; we had lost "Colin" two years ago and the prospect of Michelle's arrival filled us with both joy and trepidation. What if something would go wrong again? They hadn't detected the hole in "Colin's" lung, and when he was born it had filled with fluid. They rushed him away to Ottawa for an operation but it was too late. An agonizing memory suddenly flashed in my mind. It was Graeme entering the hospital room with flowers in his arms to visit Ruth and the new baby not knowing what had happened. When we told him he looked at Ruth with love and understanding in his eyes and said, "It's too bad. He never got to meet anybody."

Our anxieties on Michelle's account were quickly laid to rest. She was born with her eyes wide open to this new world that had just appeared around her. Her awareness gave us—and doctor Craig—quite a start.

Waiting for the train on the subway platform, my mind wandered over the billboard posters on the wall across the tracks: "Sony, the One and Only," "CFTO, Your Entertainment Network," "Night Courses at Ryerson Institute," an ad for ladies' underwear. The silence was broken by the hum of a train emerging from the far end of the tunnel. The signs were suddenly strobed by the cars flashing past. The train slowed to a halt, the doors opened, and I moved inside. As I sat down I noticed more ads above the seats across from me. You couldn't escape them. My eyes drifted down to try and catch those of the passenger across from me. However, this is Toronto. No success. My eyes glanced up again: "O'Henry," "Leave your Car at Home and Travel T.T.C." A bit redundant. If you were reading this you obviously had and did.

"Queen's Park," "St. Patrick," "Osgoode," "St. Andrew," and finally "Union Station." Escape!—once I'd finally run the gauntlet of fast food joints lining the entrance–way and manoeuvred my way through the push of commuters heading for the GO trains and their homes in the suburbs. But it was a civilised rush hour. A door held open, a thank you for doing likewise. A smile acknowledging that we we're all in this madness together. I turned right, away from the crowds of commuters and headed for the stairway to the main station, a level above. No matter how many times I passed through it, the cathedral–like marble and granite interior of the station never failed to impress, monument to an era when things were built to last. Majestic in scope, simple in design, it drew your gaze upwards toward the star–lit ceiling and beyond to the eternal. Union Station was once the hub of a network of rail lines linking the Atlantic to the Pacific, Newfoundland to Vancouver Island, and defined us as a nation. The presence of the Station seems to "announce" this to all who enter.

Today was my lucky day. VIA was on time. No long line–up

pushing people back into the station. I moved quickly on to the platform and found car 05. There was still a vacant double seat at the front end. Most times I would sit with someone and engage them in conversation to break the monotony of the journey. Today, however, I wanted some space, to enjoy the moment of Michelle's birth. No one arrived to take the seat beside me. The train moved out of the station. One stop at Guildwood in 10 minutes. My luck held. I remained alone. I had about two hours to myself before we reached Kingston. Ticket taken, I settled back in my seat to enjoy my sandwich and drink. Then I opened my notebook, pen in hand, and let my mind roam free, jotting down whatever popped up. I was feeling very relaxed and very happy.

I was thinking about how to explain what I knew of the Aboriginal way of life I had encountered in Australia on Groote Eylandt and Bickerton Island. Here were people who lived "together–apart" rather than together or apart. Unity in the sense of being or becoming "one" with others was abhorrent to them. But then so was living independently of others. It was a difficult thing to express in English. We just didn't have the words for it. Each person lived in his or her personal and social space, partly independent and partly connected to others, so the Aborigines said, through *Amawurrena* or Spiritual Substance laid down in the Creation Period—the so–called Dreamtime—each Substance different in kind from the other. So it was really Creation Substance*s* laid down in the Dreamtime. Not a common source or anything like that. From these Substances emerged lines of people who channelled their *kind* of substance over the generations through the act of reproduction. Not reproduction in our sense, though: rather a man opened up a pathway in a woman for the entrance of this Substance into her womb and the foetus growing there.

From the Substances in question emerged the different "clan" lands in the area, each with its own peculiarities and each connected to a line of people. From the Substances also emerged the different natural species, each connected to a different land and line of people. Theirs was a world of differences on all levels, each difference living in peaceful coexistence with the others. But how? Differences in my own Euro–American history inevitably seemed to lead to discrimination and violence. Ethnicity, religion, class, you name it.

Where I work in Australia, though, the Warnungamagalyuagba and Warnindilyaugwa live beside the Nunggubuyu and have done so for thousands of years, and do so without trouble. How do they do it?

I pondered this on the train. What "force" of history moved people to create differences between themselves rather than similarities and then learn to live with them? What was this "Spiritual Substance" stuff really all about?

My thoughts shifted to Sunday Morning Hockey in Perth. This is a game of ice hockey we play in the winter at the Perth arena. It's not at all like professional N.H.L. hockey—not in the way we play and not in the outcome of the games.

There's the regular five players plus a goalie on one team and five players plus a goalie on the other. One team wears Red sweaters, the other Green. We drop the puck at centre ice and play until one team scores five goals, then we switch ends but leave the goalies where they are. So, in effect, you have the Red goalie playing for the Green team and the Green goalie playing for the Red team. As in the Aboriginal case, we deny the unity of Red and the unity of Green by placing Red in Green and Green in Red. On top of that we respect each player's difference and play them at the position they are best at regardless of whether or not another player may be better at that position. We play this way each week until one team starts winning too many games then we move some of the better players from the "winningest" team over to the other until things balance out. When they do, they return to their team of origin. The result of all this is "peaceful co-existence hockey," where there is no violence and no need for referees.

My analytic mind demanded that I both try to understand and be able to explain these kinds of arrangements; my academic training provided me with a first attempt at explanation: the dialectic. The dialectic is at the basis of the Western history of ideas. It assumes that reality is, at its base, conflictual, consisting of warring opposites. Hot versus cold, black versus white, rich versus poor, me versus you, and so on. The dialectic underlies theories of history and thought from Hegel and Marx to Lévi-Strauss, from Darwin and Kant to neoconservatism. Ideas on the naturalness of the competitive market system, on the naturalness of class struggle, on the naturalness of the drive to self-sufficiency and autonomy on the part of the individual or group, all of these owe their existence to a belief in the dialectic.

The dialectic can be expressed as a process in these terms:

thesis—>antithesis—>synthesis

What this means is that something asserts itself (*thesis*), something else asserts itself against it (*antithesis*), the two struggle, one overcomes the other, or the two merge together into a unified whole (*synthesis*).

I do not question for a moment that the world often works according to the law of the dialectic. Bands merge into tribes, tribes into nations, and nations into states. People compete, classes form, violence exists. Even so, I believe that the world is *made* to work that way out of choice; it is not the only way it works or has to work. More to the point, the dialectic does not explain how the Aborigines or Sunday Morning Hockey work. Differences here do not clash, nor do they merge into larger wholes. They simply accommodate, one to the other.

Revelation?

To pass the time on the train I began to experiment with the dialectic. What if I rearranged the order of the sequence, *thesis, anti–thesis, synthesis*, would it reach a new conclusion that more resembled the Aboriginal situation or Sunday Morning Hockey?

Antithesis—>thesis—>synthesis didn't get me anywhere.

Synthesis—>thesis —>antithesis proved equally unenlightening.

Synthesis—>antithesis—>thesis was just as unpromising.

For some reason it occurred to me to substitute more concrete terms for each of these abstract formulations and try again. For instance, substituting "me," "you," and "us," for *thesis, antithesis,* and *synthesis* respectively, becomes "me first," "you second," "us" or "me over you or you over me," third. However, I got nowhere experimenting with these substitutions. So I tried even more concrete terms—particular people I know for each term. So the "me" became "myself" and the "you" became my son "Graeme." I now tried reversing the first two terms of the dialectic with "Graeme," the person, substituted for the "you," or *antithesis*, in the formulation and "I myself" substituted for *thesis,* but I never reached "I myself," or the new second term . . . .

Suddenly I was rising above myself. A feeling of awe swept over me, as if something was happening that was way beyond my comprehension. Then I was above myself in the seat, looking down on myself sitting there, notebook in hand. Then, abruptly, awe gave way to fear—a terrible gut–wrenching fear. The feeling of separation from myself on the seat was now complete. Fear dissolved and I was overwhelmed by a feeling of joy. A burden seemed to lift from my shoulders. A feeling of incredible peace swept over me. Everything I saw below me was so clear and well–defined, almost illuminated. It was like looking down on patches of oil floating on a pool of water reflecting the sunlight. I felt a presence. Then I began to move back toward my physical self on the seat. And as I did an idea came into my mind. It was the first two terms of the dialectic in reversed order followed by a new third term:

Antithesis—>thesis—>plurality (part–of–one–in–the–other)

In personal terms, "Graeme first," "me second," "part of him in me, part of me in him."

In less personal terms, "you first," "me second," "part of you in me, part of me in you."

Was this the Aboriginal situation? Was this Sunday Morning Hockey? Was this Graeme *and* I?

But there was something else about this experience that puzzled me. As the "revelation" came to mind, something told me not to tell anybody about it.

*   *   *   *

What to make of all this? Nothing like it had ever happened to me before. I had a new experience—what many would call a mystical experience—and a new idea had come out of it, but what did it mean? How could *antithesis* be a starting point? *Antithesis* in and of itself was "nothing at all," and how could the second term in my formulation, *thesis*, or something, proceed from "nothing at all?" But I had been "nothing at all" out there above my physical self. And I had come back to my physical self from "nowhere" out there. Or had I? What was that presence I felt? My own? Someone else's? Graeme's? I simply could not sort any of this out. So I compartmentalised, relegating the experience itself to the realm of imagination and fantasy, and the idea to the realm of, well, ideas.

I did tell a few people of the experience and many more of the idea, such as it was. I published it as the "Theoretical Prelude" to my book *Life Before Genesis* (New York: Peter Lang Publishing, 1985). But I never really understood either the idea or the experience that accompanied it. I ended up reducing the *antithesis* of the idea to "the threat of becoming nothing," that is, the prospect of seeing one's existence come to an end. *Thesis* then became "the assertion of self under this threat" which lead to accommodation or *plurality* with the "other" under the same threat. This way of looking at human relationships made some sense out of Sunday Morning Hockey which had, indeed, originated as a reaction against competitive–style N.H.L. hockey. In Sunday Morning Hockey each player had put his own competitive interest aside in favour of accommodating other players in the game. The game itself balanced wins and losses and maintained accommodation by literally placing a part of one team (the goalie and, occasionally, other players) in the other.

However, the idea of looking at *antithesis* as "threat" did little to explain the Australians. The origins of their way of life was lost in the mists of time so that we have no way of knowing the process of its "coming into being." Some kind of threat could have driven a small group of them south to Australia from the Indonesian archipelago many thousands of years ago, but we have no hard evidence that such a migration occurred, never mind its cause. Nor could I fathom any threat built into their way of life which might draw people together–apart in an accommodating relationship. My experience on the train, however, had given me that part–of–one–in–the–other insight, and that enabled me to entertain the following possibility regarding the Australians: Peaceful co–existence was established by taking something of your own "clan's" "stuff" which another "clan" did not have and giving it up to them. This could be a language, a man or a woman as a spouse, or a resource you owned. I knew the Warnungamagalyuagba and Warnindilyaugwa spoke the Nunggubuyu language in addition to their own and vice versa, and there was some intermarriage between them. However, perhaps there was more to it than this. Perhaps each of the "clan's" lands was resource specific in the sense of containing much more of one thing than of something else which was found elsewhere. Perhaps one's own resources were not for oneself but for others who did not have them. The problem at this point was that I hadn't asked the Aborigines about this and I had no evidence one way or the other. I would have to return to find out.

Spirit?

This was about as far as my insight on the train took me at the time—more in the direction of raising questions than of finding any answers. I returned to the Aborigines in 1986 to test out my hypotheses regarding these part–of–one–in–the–other relationships. Research confirmed that each of the "clan" lands on Bickerton Island was in fact resource–specific, though in a more complex way than I had anticipated. Each land held an abundance of a certain resource and that resource was forbidden to the people who owned the land, yams in one country, the best fishing ground in another, wild apples in a third and a permanent fresh water supply in a fourth (though here it was not so much the water itself as animals and plants associated with the water that were forbidden). In the Aboriginal mind, the resources were forbidden because they were sung by the people in question and they were sung because they were associated with the same or closely related Spiritual Substance in the Dreamtime. In fact, there was even more to it than this. It wasn't just the lands that were resource–specific but also, in a sense, the people. Nineteen–eighty–six was the year I was put through the second stage of initiation which involved participating in a mortuary ceremony for one of my "sisters" and being painted up with a ceremonial design at the climax of the ceremony. The next day the implications for myself —following from Aboriginal Law—were made explicit.

"You have nothing, everything we have is yours," Gudigba said when I met him in the camp. I had not been told this before. Perhaps I had not been ready for it. This is because the obverse is also true: "We have nothing, everything you have is ours." Indeed, they do mean everything—food, clothes, possessions of any kind, money, even your children. The Law is that when someone has nothing of something he or she is in need of, then the person who has it is obliged to give to them all of what they have of it. There is no obligation to reciprocate, there is no exchange, there is no sharing, you simply give all of it up. Conversely, if you are with nothing of it yourself, and if you are in need of it, then you have a right to all that someone else has of it. This is renunciation in its purest form. For example, if I am fishing and I spear a fish, as soon as the fish is in my possession and I bring it to shore, I must give it up to those who have no fish, first and foremost to those who in a sense have the *least* of nothing, namely young children and old people. This act of renunciation on my part, though, entitles me eventually to receive fish from someone else. The giving up of children is a little more complex.

A woman bears a child not for herself but for her husband and his sister. Aborigines say that Spiritual Substance flows down from father and sister, through father, to his children (who are, in a sense, the children of his sister even though she does not bear them, as she shares the same spiritual identity as her brother). The father's wife, the "real" mother in our sense, is simply the receptacle within which the child is formed. Indeed, it is questionable whether the father is even the father in our sense, since his role is simply to open up in his wife a pathway through which a spirit–child, originating in the same Spiritual Substance as he and his sister, can enter the foetus. The physical constitution of the foetus is of no consequence to the Aborigines and they do not overly ponder as to how it comes to be or how it might affect the child's appearance and behaviour (something we appear to be obsessed with).

Part–of–one–in–the–other relationship, then, is effected by a process of "expelling" to and from "nothing" in the sense of "the absence of something." But how could "nothing" in and of itself cause the giving up? If renunciation had a deeper basis, something that compelled its practice apart from enforcement of the Law, I did not at this point know what it was.

What I did realise at this point is that realities—ways of life—do exist which are not founded on binary discrimination, class or ethnic conflict, or fundamental schism. Differences can exist to link people rather than divide them. Indeed, the Aboriginal way of life *requires* an endless creation of differences in order to make peaceful co–existence and mutual accommodation work. For without difference you have nothing to renounce. This is because the difference that I have is for you, whether this be a resource, a possession I own, or a skill or ability I possess. Women gather, men hunt in Aboriginal society so that each has something to provide the other whether or not each could provide both hunting and gathering resources for themselves.

If we are each autonomous and self-sufficient as an individual, group, nation, then we have nothing that the other needs. Here our "difference" is a barrier between us that defines you as you and me as me and neither of us in need of each other.

By placing a part of oneself in the other, whether it be self as such, the services one provides, or the things one possesses, one transcends division, separation, and duality, and one undermines *the* fundamental source of conflict and violence in the world.

In 1986 I learned something else from the Aborigines. We place a part of ourselves in the other almost inadvertently as we proceed through life. In every place we visit, in every person we meet, we leave something of our *Amawurrena* or Spiritual Substance. This is why, when someone dies, the Aborigines take the spirit of the dead person on a journey to all the places it has been while in bodily form. It is to collect up the residue of their Spiritual Substance and send it over to them before they go on to their final resting place. This is why those closest to the deceased are kept in a state of relative seclusion. It is so that the Spiritual Substance of the deceased that remains with them can be carried away on the smoke of fires lit for the purpose to join the deceased. The person's house is smoked for the same reason. The things persons had in their possession when they died are also burned for the same reason. Then the Aborigines sing and remember for up to five years until the last of the residue of the person's Spiritual Substance has dissipated.

Spiritual Substance itself is the original "stuff" of creation and, when "activated" (*alawuduwarra*), is a force for forming the multiplicity of animate and inanimate life. Spiritual Substance as a person's inner spirit is called *amugwa* and is housed inside the body, below the naval. This is the spirit that travels to "this side" on birth and to the "other side" on death. Spiritual Substance as a person's outer spirit is called *awarrawalya* and is visible (at least to Aborigines) as one's "illuminated presence" or "Form." This aspect connects through to the "other side" and "channels" one's *amugwa* to and from there at birth and death.

On the death of a person his or her *amugwa* is accompanied across to the "other side" by musicians and songmen on the sound of the didjeridu and voice where it is left to proceed further by itself once it is certain it *will* proceed. This is determined by the extent to which the mourners are able to control their grief. If the spirit senses its loss is too much to bear for those left behind, it will not go on but remain with them until they have dealt with it. If the spirit and the mourners successfully make their respective transitions, the performers pick up the ancestral spirits from the "other side" and guide them back to where they are currently gathered to bear witness that they are maintaining their traditions. This is when the burning of the possessions takes place. Then, some time later, they go over again for the deceased's spirit and take it on the "clean–up" journey mentioned above. On these occasions, then, both the spirits of the dead and the spirits of the living are "over there," together on the "other side."

Was it the *amugwa* of myself I had sensed outside my body that day on the train? Was it the *awarrawalya* of myself, that illuminated presence, I had seen of myself sitting on the seat? I wasn't sure.

That was about to change.

PART II

A:NELANGWA, HIS SPIRIT LIVES

2

54 DRUMMOND ST. WEST

I remember the last time I saw Iain alive as if it were yesterday. It was March 5, 1988, a Saturday. I had driven down from Toronto to my parents home in Perth (photo 2) and Iain was there waiting for me when I arrived. As I came in the door and said, "Hi, Iain," he jumped off the couch and came running over to me with his arms outstretched. I reached down and picked him up and drew him close to my chest. As I did he put his arms around my neck, his cheek on mine, and hugged me. But this time something different happened. He began to pat me on the shoulder with his right hand. I realised he was comforting me. He was feeling my pain, my inability to deal with the inevitable. The inevitable was that he was leaving. It was his way of saying "It's all right. It's going to be all right now for both of us."

He died on Tuesday as Ruth was driving him to Sick Children's Hospital in Ottawa. Fortunately for me I was in Dr. Oxlade's office in Kingston on my way back to Toronto when the news came through. Otherwise I don't know what I would have done. I loved that little boy more than my own life.

*   *   *   *

Nineteen eighty–six, two years before, had been the most rewarding year of my working life. I had returned to Australia to work with the Northern Territory and federal governments establishing local government institutions for Aboriginal people in the Territory. I had spent some six months on Groote Eylandt and Bickerton Island with my family, living with the Aborigines, testing and confirming my hypotheses, and going through the second stage of initiation. I returned home to Canada on an emotional and intellectual high. Within a week our lives had plummeted to their lowest depths. It all happened so fast it seemed like a dream.

We took Iain to hospital in Ottawa on the Friday of the Labour Day weekend for some tests to diagnose what we thought might be a virus he had picked up in Australia complicated by jet lag. Iain seemed to have withdrawn into himself and had become so disoriented he could not walk unassisted. I went back to Perth for the weekend while the tests were being analysed, and then I left for Toronto on Monday to begin preparations for the teaching year. On Wednesday night Ruth phoned me in my room at Trinity College where I stayed during the week. She cautioned me to sit down. Then she told me the news. It wasn't a virus. It was neuroblastoma, a form of childhood cancer. Iain had been diagnosed at stage four. Stage five is death. The cancer had spread throughout his body. It was choking him and was pressing on his optic nerve. He was virtually blind. There was no hope, he had but a few days to live. I was to pick up Graeme and Michelle in Perth and bring them to Ottawa to say good–bye.

I didn't know what to do, I felt so helpless. So I did what I hadn't done since childhood, I prayed. I knelt before my bed that night but instead of invoking a deity for help I reached deep inside myself and tried to project myself to Iain. I really didn't know what I was doing or why. It was just something I did. After I don't know how long—maybe an hour or two, maybe more—I found myself sitting up on top of my bed with a strange disembodied sensation, as if I was floating back to myself, much like my experience on the train. Then I felt this overwhelming sense of relief and fell asleep.

The next day I drove to Perth and picked up the kids. Iain hadn't spoken since entering hospital. He had just lain there with Ruth beside him, clinging to her, frightened. As the tumour expanded it was pushing on his internal organs and you could see them pressing against his skin. His body was becoming so sensitive to touch that Ruth could do little more than hold his hand. As we entered the room Graeme and Michelle said something to him and suddenly the body on the bed came alive and sat up and started talking back. What was happening? No one was quite sure. The nurses rushed in. There was a moment of confusion, some time to regroup, and then Iain was transported away for some new tests. The tumour had suddenly and inexplicably stopped spreading. No one could explain it. Even the doctors called it a miracle. Well, maybe, maybe not.

What I was doing to reach him from Toronto, Ruth was doing beside him in Ottawa. And Graeme and Michelle's presence certainly triggered something dramatic in him. However, these aren't the kinds of things you can tell doctors unless you're willing to risk being labelled crazy. So I kept them to myself.

Almost immediately the cancer began to recede. For the doctors this was their window of opportunity. Now they could apply their own claims to cure, namely chemotherapy, radiation treatment, drug cocktails. I thought then and still think today that if we had just let well enough alone and let Iain proceed with curing himself, he would still be alive. The thing was, Iain was a stage four neuroblastoma who had lived—the first at this hospital. According to the statistics, a stage four has only a 2% chance of survival. They wanted to see if their methods could beat these odds. But he had already beat the odds! He was a stage four, alive, and going into remission.

Ruth and I debated between ourselves what to do and then we debated with the doctors. Finally, the doctors called us to a meeting at Sick Children's. Bluntly and without any consideration for our opinion they said, "If we don't intervene and Iain dies it will be your fault." It was intimidation and we gave in to it. Well, they did intervene, and he did die. It follows from their line of argument that it was their fault. But they never assumed any responsibility: "His chances were only 2% anyway," they consoled us.

With treatment, Iain was in and out of remission for the next 18 months. He lost his red hair and when it came back between treatments it was black. He retained only about 10% of his vision and only in one eye, and yet he learned to read, hit a baseball, and play games. His courage was phenomenal. A joy to everyone he met, always a smile and occasionally this enlivening chuckle that originated way deep down in his being and resonated throughout his entire body. He loved the autumn leaves in all their multicoloured splendour. He loved playing in them under the old maple tree at the end of the lane where we waited for Graeme and Michelle to return from school. He loved riding with me on the lawn tractor, touching the animals, feeling the warm summer breeze. He loved life more than anyone I have ever known. However, while he was motoring on, we were slowly coming apart around him, the dread of those odds forever in the backs of our minds.

Iain knew who he was and where he had come from. It was unnerving.

One afternoon while I was typing away at my desk composing a book called *Return to Eden* about our experiences with the Aborigines in 1986 Iain came to see me. It was his book, I was writing it for him, a special part of myself for him, and he knew this. He would often come and just stand there watching or sit on my lap as I typed around him. Often I would ask him about the things he remembered living with the Aborigines—learning some of the language, having a "clan," knowing his totems. But this time it was he who began to talk. I must admit, at first I wasn't paying a lot of attention.

"Dad," he said, "This is what it was like before I was born." He doubled over into the foetal position. "It was dark and quiet but I could hear," he went on. Now he had my attention. However, before I could reorient myself he was walking away and when I caught up to him to question him further, it was gone.

One lunch time as Ruth was doing the dishes, Iain came up to her and began tugging on her dress. She, too, wasn't paying much attention. Then he started to talk about riding on a horse in a town somewhere—something about cobblestones I think. At first she thought he was recounting a story, or something on T.V., but then she realised he was talking about himself as an adult being somewhere in some other time and place. By the time she had gathered her wits together enough to ask him more about it, it was gone.

A remarkable little guy, an "old soul" as a friend of mine described him. He died on March 8, 1988, and is buried beneath a maple tree looking out over farmers' fields to a lake in the United Church cemetery near Rideau Ferry where we used to attend church.

Aftermath

Shortly after his death we received a letter from Bobby Nunggumajbarr on behalf of the Angurugu Aboriginal Council on Groote Eylandt. It read,

Dear David and Ruth & Family,

The President, Town Clerk and Councillors of the Angurugu Community Government Council would like to express our sympathy to you and your family on behalf of the Wanindilyakwa people of Groote Eylandt, on the death of your little son Iain.

We remember that little boy living here and you must be very sad that he has died.

We are looking forward to seeing you when you come back here during this year and we can talk to you then.

Yours Sincerely and with Sympathy,

This letter meant a lot to us. Iain had touched their lives as he had touched ours and they had taken the time and trouble to tell us so. And at a time when their own troubles made ours pale by comparison. Many of the Aborigines were dying from a mysterious neurological degenerative disease in which the body painfully wastes away around the nervous system over a period of years. Alcoholism and violence were rampant in the community. Manganese mining was ravaging the landscape. I wanted to go back and help in the aftermath of Iain's death, but I couldn't.

The summer following Iain's death I made it as far as Darwin and just sat there unable to move. They knew I was there and never really understood why I didn't show up. I'm not sure I do. There was just this heavy weight of failure sitting on my shoulders. I hadn't been able to save him, or my family, or myself. I had lost confidence in my abilities, in my self as a person and I guess I just didn't want anyone to see.

I returned home from Australia to find another letter which began to put things in perspective for me. It was from Mildred Healey, a member of a sister United Church in our charge.

Dear David,

Please accept my apologies in being so long sending you our sincere sympathy in the passing of your little son Iain. Certainly his time of illness was a most painful time for you. While there's life there's hope and no doubt you were clinging to the hope that Iain might be healed. Apparently this was not God's will and our Faith tells us that 'God's way is the Best Way.' Since God saw fit to take Iain in his arms to be with Him, you can take comfort in knowing that, for Iain, it is now much better as he is now free from all pain and knows only Peace and Joy, right?

Also we are deeply saddened that you and Ruth are not together at the present time. Stress of any kind usually takes its toll on a marriage, and I should think that nothing might be more destructive to a husband–wife relationship than the lingering illness and death of a child. Time does heal, we're often told, and for you, David, I'm praying that time, with God's help, will heal all the wounds that are presently causing you much distress. Many times thus far in my life I've wished I could re–live some past experiences and handle them differently than I did. However, this opportunity is not given to us. So we must pick up the pieces, face the future and, with God's Help, strive to follow His leading.

May God bless you, David, enrich your life both physically and spiritually and grant you His peace—now and always. Should there be anything I could do to help in any way, please don't hesitate to let me know.

Sincerely,

God hath not promised we shall not know
Toil and temptations, trouble and woe,
He hath not told us we shall not bear
Many a burden, many a care.
But God hath promised strength for the day
Rest for the labour, light for the way,
Grace for the trials, help from above,
Unfailing kindness, undying love.

It was a simple expression of faith from someone I knew only casually. It assumed a common frame of reference which, in fact, I did not really share. However, it moved me deeply and brought one thing in particular to mind. The issue of control. I wanted to be in control. However, even when I thought I was in control such as that night at Trinity College when I reached out to Iain, I wasn't in control. I had simply opened myself up to a possibility and it had happened. Why it happened may have had little to do with me. Other forces outside my control may have been at work. How arrogant to think that *I* could save him. My whole approach to life, to those close to me, was wrong. It was something I had to let go of. I had to change.

*   *   *   *

I remember the first time I saw Iain after he died. It was in my parents' home in Perth the following evening. I was sitting on the couch in the living room looking at nothing in particular and feeling kind of empty and drained when a shimmer of light—not really light, but more a translucence—moved in front of me from left to right. It had no real shape—no fixed shape in any case—but it had form. It moved above the floor sort of suspended in space, and I knew it was Iain. I just *knew*. Then it vanished as it neared the fireplace at the end of the living room. I felt shocked, jolted into awareness. It took my breath away. In the months after the funeral, though, I pushed the experience to the back of my mind. Finally, I denied it.

3

TRINITY COLLEGE

The second time I saw Iain after he died was in my room at Trinity College in November of 1988. The events leading up to this experience, and which involved me only indirectly, were as unsettling as the event itself and I want to recount them in all their detail. They involve two people I will call Kate and Ellen as both wish to remain anonymous. Kate was an old acquaintance of mine from Toronto who now lived in Australia. Ellen was a friend of hers who lived in New Zealand. Ellen, though, had been born in Australia of a white father and an Aboriginal mother. She had migrated to New Zealand with her husband where she worked with Maori people.

Passing through Toronto shortly after Iain died, Kate called to say hello and we met briefly at the University before she left to return to Australia. She knew I had lost a son and she expressed her condolences, saying that if I needed any help dealing with it, she had this friend Ellen who might be able to help. I wasn't sure what kind of help she meant since Ellen was far away in New Zealand, so I asked her. Ellen was a seer, she said. She could make connections with "the other side," and she had great compassion and understanding. I thought to myself, "I really don't believe in that kind of thing," but out of respect for Kate's kindness I replied, "Well, I guess it couldn't do any harm." She left and I thought no more about it, not, at least, until I received the following letter dated October 16th, 1988.

Dear David,

I did enjoy our lunch and talk together. I have been thinking about some of the things you have had to keep inside and your experiences with traditional Aboriginals which may not always be understood or tolerated by others. As I am seeing Ellen I will ask her about your son, or both your children who have gone on before you. It may not be necessary, but if you have something small which belonged to your son could you send it to me in NZ. This helps her. I detach myself from this process as it really hasn't anything to do with me. But she is a kind person, with exceptional wisdom—and you have had a long association with Aboriginals. I will see what I can do for you. You must expect the message to be small, if one comes. But it may help you put all that has happened to you in recent years in perspective. I would do this willingly as a friend. (A small toy, clothing, or any other thing will do. I will return it to you.)

Kind regards,

I replied:

Oct. 25/88

Dear Kate,

Thanks so much for your note and the thought. I have sent you the last thing Iain made for me before he died. It is a paper bird [cover]. I love him so much.

David

She replied:

5.11.88

Dear David,

I just received your letter today with the lovely little bird made by your son. I had written last week to Ellen to let her know I would be coming to see her when I arrive on the 22nd Nov. After receiving your letter I wanted to make sure she would be there, so I telephoned her this afternoon.

It is always wonderful to be with Ellen, for me she is a means by which I recharge my batteries. I get very battered in my work from many quarters, and she has a way of putting the essence of life into perspective.

I told her a little about you, and your work in Australia. I also told her that you had sent your son's little bird. She said to me that you were 'very brave' to send me this, knowing that it was the last thing he made for you, David.

I also told Ellen something I experienced, while we were talking over lunch. But which I did not tell you, as I thought at the time, you would probably not believe me. She said I should have told you. So I feel I had better do so now.

While we were talking about your son I suddenly felt a presence at your left shoulder (I have felt presences of my own relatives on and off since I was a child. For many years my father's mother would come and visit me when I was a little girl. She died in childbirth when my father was 13 yrs and had lost her little girl. I expect she was fond of me). I have no doubt of the experience David. Your son is very close to you, I would expect at all times. He was standing behind you and slightly to your left.

Ellen's response to this on the phone to me is that your great sorrow is keeping your child 'earth bound.' He must also love you very much and cannot tear himself away. He needs to be released in order that he can go on. As you need help in your sorrow, he may also need help.

Ellen will do a reading for you. And I expect she will also ask for help for you and your son. I will take notes of what she says and send these to you. But if you want to feel a part of this I will give you the time. We will do this on 22 Nov. at one o'clock in the afternoon. As NZ is 18 hrs ahead of Toronto this will be at (21 Nov.) 7 pm Monday evening for you. You may like to find somewhere quiet to meditate at that time. It will take about 30 minutes.

Do not be afraid. You may not, necessarily, experience anything at that time. If you do, it will not be frightening, it may even be peaceful.

Your child has experienced enough pain in this world, you must, out of love, allow him the joys and growth of the next world, David. You must also accept his passing with love and acceptance, that he can feel able to leave you and prepare a place for you when it is your time. But your time is not now. You have more to do here yet.

The full meaning of the short life of your son and your broken marriage may not become apparent to you immediately, it will come to you in wisdom and with time—and the fullness of that meaning will not be revealed until the next world. But understanding and acceptance will come, nonetheless, when you let him go. I am sure that both you and he will receive help to do this. It is best for both your sakes, though terribly painful. Be assured that you are not alone David. Ellen, I and many others who you may not realise will help you.

Kindest regards,

Kate was right. If she had told me she sensed Iain's presence with me at the time I would not have believed her. I really did not believe her now. I thought she was just trying to comfort me. However, I would do what they asked on the 21st and have a quiet time by myself.

Before that day came, however, I had a dream. At least I think it was a dream. It was so vivid I wasn't sure if I was asleep or awake. It was of Iain's countenance but his features were far more vivid and clear than in life. The top of his head—his hair—was red and shining. The hair around the side, though, was black. In my dream he somehow seemed much older, but it was still Iain at the age of five.

On Monday evening about 6:30 p.m. I returned to my apartment at Trinity College, intending to open a bottle of red wine, break some bread, and perform my own little communion while whatever was going on in New Zealand was going on. But when I tried to pull the cork out of the bottle with my corkscrew it wouldn't budge. Then I did the funniest thing. I stopped, stood there and simply asked out loud for the cork to be removed. Pulling ever so gently on the corkscrew, it slipped out. I poured the wine into a glass and broke the bread. Then I ate the bread and drank the wine and went into the living room, turned on some classical music, and sat down on the couch. I was just sitting there not thinking about anything when my eyes lifted and focused on the painting of Stony Lake near Peterborough which hung on the wall opposite me. It used to hang on the wall of our log home in North Burgess Township (photo 4) near Perth, and Iain and I would often sit there and look at it while we listened to music or just spent time together. It had been painted by Ken McClelland a neighbour of my parents in Perth, and he had given it to me shortly before he died. He was in his early 90s.

Slowly I found myself being drawn into the picture. Then I realised I was looking at Iain in the reflection of the glass—or rather in the lake and the trees on the other side of the glass. It wasn't really an image of Iain but rather that same translucence I had seen before at my parents'. I sat there, mesmerised. The whole scene started coming alive. The trees were swaying as if in a wind, waves were rolling over the lake and on to the shore. And then I began to weep. Not because I was unhappy, or happy either for that matter. They were tears of equal proportions of sorrow and joy. I realised I had reached a moment of truth. Could I let him go or not? I felt a sharp pain in my heart, yet a sense of security knowing what had to be done. I started to speak: "You can go, I'll be all right," I kept saying, over and over again. I was weeping. Then I remembered the way we used to be together on the couch and I stretched out and held my arms as if to cradle him. Suddenly, I swear he was there, in my arms, just for an instant. Then I began to speak again, but this time, something different: "I'll stay, I'll stay, I won't go," I kept repeating. Then I realised what I was saying. Deep down inside me I wanted to go over and join him just so he wouldn't be lonely. As soon as this dawned on me he was gone, and I was just sitting on the couch looking at a painting of Stony Lake. It was at that moment that I remembered the real name of the son we had lost 10 years earlier. It was Bryan. I had been referring to him as Colin all these years, and no one had corrected me. (Colin was to have been his name but it had been given to the child of close friends of ours so we changed it to Bryan.) I got up, went into the bathroom and washed my face. It was 10 minutes to 7. Then I came back into the living room and sat down on the couch. But something in me told me I had to go over to Trinity College chapel (photo 6). So

I put on coat and boots and headed across the quad.

The chapel was dark as I entered and sat in the first seat I came to. I was feeling very relaxed, if a bit exhausted. I was thinking to myself, "He's gone," when I looked up at the vaulted ceiling to see a little flicker of light pass along its length, give a little burst, and then vanish. I sat silently by myself for a while and then got up and left. It was 7:30.

When I returned to my apartment later that evening, I wrote to Ellen through Kate and told her exactly what had just happened. I mailed the letter the next morning.

Ellen's reading had proceeded, though not quite as planned. Unexpected things had begun happening around Ellen before the reading took place and before Kate arrived and these puzzled her. Ellen wrote down these happenings herself as she was fully conscious of them. The events of the reading, however, were written down by Kate as Ellen recounted them while in a kind of trance. Of these Ellen has no memory. Then they put the readings in an envelope and the next day mailed them to me in Canada. In other words, our two reports crossed in the mail. So there is no possibility of reinterpretation after the event.

What Kate told me much later is that she did not tell Ellen my name, nor that I had lost another son ten years earlier, only that I was a friend of hers, had lost a child whose paper bird she now had, and that I had worked for a long time with Aboriginal people in Australia. Nor did Kate herself know where I lived near Perth or even that I lived near Perth. She had left Toronto some years before I moved there. Nor did she know I had lived in a cottage on Otty Lake (photo 3) at the time Bryan died.

First Kate's letter accompanying the readings:

22nd Nov. 1988

Dear David,

Ellen picked me up at the airport. She was half an hour late. 'The reason,' she told me in the car going to her place, 'was that she was being 'followed around all morning by two boys.' They kept scattering leaves all around. Beautiful autumn leaves. They just spread them around and then scooped them up in very little piles. 'I told them that I had to finish my vacuuming, but they wouldn't go away.'

Then she explained that these two boys had 'been with her since about Sunday (Nov. 19th) at 6:30 p.m. There was so much light around them,' she said, 'it was difficult to tell their ages.' (Ellen explains, the people in Spirit continue to grow spiritually. That is, from what I understand, there is an appearance of this growth or maturation in their spiritual presence.) They often tell you how old they were when they passed over. Only you will know from her description. For instance, she talks to you of two boys—one who was older and one younger. She seemed to think that the younger one was about eight years old when he passed over. But the older 'taller' one, she said had such light around him it was 'hard to tell his age.'

From what I can tell it was the younger one who spoke most to you. But the older one sent you beautiful balls of light. (Pink light, Ellen has told me before, represent the light of love. I do not know what the other colours mean. You will have to ask her.) Ellen said the boys 'were very close' (to each other). 'There was a woman hovering in the background, a distance away. Someone looking after them.' It would seem that this woman had brought them and was waiting to take them back.

Ellen eventually had to stop what she was doing and sit down to listen to the boys. The cards which I have enclosed is the reading which she received that morning before she met me. I said to her that it seemed they were impatient to talk with her and hardly needed me, with your letter and your son's little bird. She said 'once the connection has been made—this is all that's needed.'

'There was so much light around them,' she said again, 'they are on a very high plane.' 'When they left,' she said, 'they left together taking these beautiful leaves with them.' And she waved her hands in an upward scooping motion. Her images described in these readings are the most beautiful I have ever heard from Ellen. They must be very, very special David. They are full of love and grace.

I asked her: 'Does this mean that David has let them go, even before we met?' 'Yes,' she said. [Kate thought that it might have something do with me receiving her letter of the 5th of November.]

I can only understand from this conversation that the boys were impatient to speak with Ellen from that moment of release David. I am relating everything that I can to you, so you may make sense of it for yourself. I will keep no copy of these notes.

I also enclose the original and early drafts of the reading which we still conducted at 1 p.m. as we said we would for you. I do not feel it is appropriate that I throw these away. I have typed these out and added comments and a few small things which I still remembered but did not actually write down at the time. But on the whole this is exactly as I recorded the happenings.

Before you read the script below you must read the cards which I enclose. This was Ellen's morning reading, when she was in the company of your boys. And this conversation is referred back to in the afternoon session. It is therefore important that you read the cards first so you understand the later references. Note that there are four sides to the cards. Read them in order.

You must keep in mind that I told Ellen very little about you and that there are aspects of your life which I do not even know myself, nor have I ever met any member of your family. I had not even told her your name before I arrived. In the morning's reading which she gave me immediately on her arrival at her house, she said the letter "T" had come through. She felt this referred to your name. You will see this on the cards. I certainly didn't tell her that you were 'looking to the past' for understanding in your work. Yet you will see this reoccurs in the early and later readings. I think this is particularly significant for you! If there are things here which are particularly true or relevant it is, according to Ellen, 'Spirit's way of reassuring you that it is genuine.'

I hope that this is a turning point in your life for you, as I believe it is meant to be. These messages are precious. They may not come again. Nor should they be particularly sought for their own sakes. They are special gifts in time of need and could give you strength for many years. There will be things said here that will have special meaning to you alone. They probably should not be shared with others who may not understand. Some things will even not become apparent to you for some time.

Ellen also said that she thought it was a pity that I did not bring you with me. She felt that a visit in person to her would 'help your growth,' and she hoped that you would visit her one day. I said I would relate this to you. If you would like to write and thank her for the reading, her address is . . . .

Please use your knowledge of Ellen with discretion. She is a limited resource and should not be spread around indiscriminately. She is, in fact, a fairly well guarded secret—kept from the public and the press for her own safety. It is a blessing to have met her.

When you read the script below you will see there are different speakers. The key to these are at the beginning. Have these clearly in your mind before proceeding.

God Bless, David

(No money must be offered to her, she is a 'seer' not a commercial spiritualist. She is recognised as such in the Maori world—and those Europeans who know her well. If you would like to give her something, a copy of one of your special books on the Aboriginal people would be an appropriate gift. You will remember that she is an Aboriginal woman. If you visit her, gifts of food are also acceptable.)

The First Reading, Tuesday Morning November 22

> Being shown a grey/green fir tree with small cones on the ends of small branches [a small drawing follows]. It has green grass around it when the cones drop. A tree that one would find out standing in a forest situation, it glows with light. One would get great strength from it. Have 3 paper balls, a daisy with a very bright yellow centre being given from Spirit. A rock being shown [small drawing follows]. Clay colours with ribs of granite through it. Four very old dark gentlemen sitting with legs crossed in a [drawing of a square with a dot signifying a person at its upper right corner.] [This person] has a wispy beard, he has 2 or 3 teeth missing. On right side a small mole on side of nostril. These men are keepers of the LAND. Have two young boys in Spirit, hard to tell their ages as they have very strong light around them. The tall one is here in front of me with lots of autumn leaves all over my carpet and he's standing in the middle of them smiling. He has lovely white teeth, a hole in the left toe of his sneakers, was very fond of these shoes. He is saying I am safe with Dream Time People. You, T or Tee, have much work to do, many lands to walk—many pages to write—the Reward is Within—the children are awaiting your (turn) return—take out the volume again, that you have put in the dark. Looks like a cupboard under a staircase, smells a bit. I am Safe, it's beautiful. Gramps is here too and Charlie and Jessie. The boy is showing me a baby deer and a short man with a hand made bow, he is very still watching the deer, the snow is melting, very peaceful. Now it's green. Gwendelyne—May. A house is very clear, but it is taken away and replaced with an orange blue tent. Home is where the Heart Is. Walk tall in the knowledge that I am Safe in the light of love—get on with your work. Happy Birthday.
>
> The smaller Boy was 8 when he passed over, the taller one I couldn't tell he is so light (must have been very special on this side). He is giving me Pink, mauve, purple and pale blue & green, balls of light to pass on to you. A huge orange ball, like the Sun going down in the desert (it's beautiful) Spain? (the word). Old fashion coaches in miniature being repainted. 7. off. Look to the past for the new beginning. All's well.

My mind sought immediately for referents. Of course it did, and, of course, they can always be found. Readings such as this are usually so general that almost anything can be read into them. However, a number of specifics here stood out. It was hard to ignore the "7. off"—precisely the time my experience of Iain in my room at Trinity came to an end. Furthermore, Ellen encountered two boys, not one—Ellen did not know we had lost two children. But neither had passed over at the age of eight—Iain was five when he died and Bryan had been only a week or so old. He would have been 10 had he lived.

But then she was right that one was much older than the other, though how "older" and "younger" works in "spirit–time" is not entirely clear.

Then there was the tree—the first image in the reading. We had planted a fir tree in front of the log house in North Burgess Township where we lived when Iain was born (photo 4). It was the *only* tree in front of the house and it was Iain's tree. At Christmas we put lights on it. It really did shine. Then the granite. The house was part of what in Lanark County is known as a rock farm. Ruggedly beautiful to look at it but not much good for farming. More granite than soil and grass. Then the mention of autumn leaves in the reading—something very special to Iain. The four, dark, old men, keepers of the land, could be four Aboriginal people I worked with in 1969. Galiyawa (photo 34), the one closest to me, had the English name Charlie. Four is the base–number of the society—the minimum number of "clans" it takes to make the marriage system work. Deer? Yes, we would see them out in front of the farmhouse all the time. Archer? No. Perhaps long ago before the white man came. The "T," of course, is me. And that's about as far as it goes.

The Second Reading, Tuesday November 22, 1 p.m.

Key: Ellen = E; Spirit = S; Recorder = K

E: This person (David) has a problem with his throat. He gets so het up, he can't say those things that are deep down in him. They get caught in his throat.
K: (Ellen puts her hand to her throat and looks troubled.)
K: (Ellen often becomes the state of the person(s) she is meditating for, in this case you David. From the beginning you are included in this reading as if you are there with us.)
E: —raspy, swollen glands. This man is out of balance. He sits with his hands on his right shoulder. He thinks. He is always asking 'Why?'
K: (Ellen takes out the bird from the letter.)
E: Isn't that so beautiful—spiritual, that he should make his father a bird!
K: (Ellen holds it between her hands.)
E: So much warmth in it.
S: "Walk the path that is awaiting you."
E: It is so clear.
S: "I forgot the eye."
K: (Ellen looks at the bird.)
E: It hasn't got an eye in it. There is such warmth in it.

S: "Thirteen months is long enough."

E: Does this mean that it has been 13 months since he passed?

K: "I don't know."

E: This must go back to him.

K: (meaning the bird to David.)

E: Does this man (David) live near a huge, is it a Sycamore, tree?

K: (Ellen is not sure of the kind of tree.)

E: I am being shown a big dark tree. Do they lose their leaves?

S: "He passes it every day."

K: (It would seem that this tree was a special or favourite of the child's, or something that he noticed and remembered.)

E: My throat has gone now.

K: (meaning the soreness/tension in her/David's throat.)

S: "Meridian"

E: I am getting the word "Meridian." What does that mean?

K: (Ellen looks at the bird again.)

E: That's wonderful for him to keep. There is great love and warmth in it for him.

E: What is a whole lot of men with pigtails mean? You know, plaits, down their back from the nape of the neck—thirteen of them.

K: "I don't know, it may be Indian."

E: A preparation for something.

K: (This may be symbolic of the thirteen months of grieving.)

E: I see a beautiful tan and white horse with sturdy legs. On a cliff top. A strong Indian Chief sits on top of him.

S: "Of times gone by."

E: He has a breast plate of feathers and stones.

K: (She describes it by drawing on her breast with her fingers—as the picture below shows.)

> ^^^ rows of turquoise for strength
> ^^^ garnets
> ^^^ feathers
> ^^^ stones collected, woven and
> > < plaited to keep in place

E: He (the chief) has a high head gear. Has a rainbow above his head. He is looking out.

K: (presumably over plains from a clifftop.)

S: "Be still and you will see forever."

K: (Spirit becomes agitated and wants to tell Ellen so much. She asks him to 'tell her one thing at a time.' He wants to show her the beauty of what he sees.)

E: (to Spirit): "Yes, I know, it's brilliant. Especially as the sun goes down."

K: (Ellen uses his words here, as this is what he wishes to communicate.)

E: David is having trouble with his left ear. This chief speaks to him into his left ear but he (David) is deaf to it. He thinks he has a pain in the ear.

S: "Carnegal."

K: (We think this is a place in America of which he speaks—we are not sure of the spelling, but this is as it sounds.)

S: —seventeeth century—a time when one could see forever.

K: (Then a whole message comes from the chief, it comes very fast and I have to write quickly. I rewrite it immediately afterwards so it is not forgotten. The words are exactly as they came. This man appears your special guide and helper David.)

"Do not be afraid to walk the path of life
Even though you are ridiculed by others.
They do not understand.
Walk tall, be proud
For I am with you
You are not alone.
May the sun always shine on your forehead
And the strength be with your soul."

E: They're gone now. Oh, that was lovely. I wish you could see it. He'll (David) be OK now.

K: (We have a break for about 20 minutes, at which time I write out again from the notes a second draft. Then your son comes back.)

S: "You can put the eye in for me."

K: (He instructs Ellen to write this message to you on your letter. Ellen does this for you. She looks at the bird again.)

E: How symbolically spiritual a bird is. To all people a bird is so free and so simple, so intelligent. To all cultures there is always a bird that is special.

K: (Other spirits come now.)

E: This volume.

K: (she refers to the first message which she got with the visit of your two sons in the morning.)

S: "The time is right to bring it out now.
He knows the time is right.
His whole being knows.
He feels he will be ridiculed.
It is the written word, the written word."

E: It must have been there a long time if the cupboard is musty smelling.

E: I feel what David has been through is a preparation for what is to come.

S: "He's had an awful lot of garbage spat at him."

K: (Ellen seems startled by the intensity of this statement.)

S: "By people who don't understand.
So bad it's venomous—really they are jealous—
That is their own fear."

E: I am being shown a scholar's hat with a cerise (cherry red) tassel.
A woman is wearing it.

S: "A lot of pain has gone into obtaining it."

E: This woman is quite plump, large hips. About five foot one and a half, I suppose.

K: "Is this person in spirit?"

E: Not in spirit.

K: (I do not know David but could this be referring to your wife and what she has suffered in the years she gave you moral support? You will have to interpret this yourself.)

E: I'm being shown two loafs of bread. They are being brought together by a lady's large hands—the top of her little finger on her left hand is gone. Her pans are very old. One has a large hole in it. She is telling me that she has to put 2 layers of brown paper to . . .

S: "stop the dough from popping through."

K: (This other woman is in spirit, she is just one of those who have gathered to speak to you. They sometimes tell small pieces of their own lives. We are not told of her relationship to you, if any. She has just come in friendship, as the others have.)

S: "The Dead Sea."

E: I am being shown a rock floating on the top. It's about three feet in diameter. It is the same rock I was shown before.

K: (in the morning reading.)

E: But the scars of granite have grown. It is the same rock as this morning. It means growth.

K: "If the scars of granite represent strength does this mean that David has grown in strength since this morning?"

E: Yes, it may mean this.

S: "Look to the past for your future."

E: David gets headaches up the back of his neck. These are caused by total frustration. He is a very frustrated person. There is so much he wants to do. He is fearful of letting it out.

E: Has he got a beard?

K: "Yes" (I had given her no description of you.)

E: Is it scruffy around the ears?

K: (Ellen also draws her hand down her chin.)

S: "He should trim it up."

E: He hurries in opening and shutting doors—his whiskers catch.

S: "He's not really taking care of himself at all."

S: "Spirinda"

E: Is it a word?

K: (we can't find it in the dictionary and don't know how to spell it. It is spelled here as it sounds.)

S: "An old word."

E: You will have to look it up in an old dictionary.

K: (We don't know what this means.)

K: The next day, when Ellen and I are out together, we see a tree —just like the one she drew for you on the cards. It has the little cones on it as she described. She said this is like the tree she saw in her vision. I took photos of this tree and will send these to you when they are developed

David in a couple of weeks. Ellen felt this was a confirmation to you. We had to drive from Auckland to Hamilton (about an hour and a half to two hour drive) to see such a tree. It was certainly an unusual coincidence. The second reference to a tree in the afternoon could refer to a different tree.

This reading was complicated by Kate's presence and her occasional intervention as interpreter. She had her own frame of reference, and there was the very real danger that she would shift the direction in which Ellen was going. Take, for instance, the Indian Chief. That began simply with Ellen's vision of thirteen men with pigtails. But Kate commented, "I don't know, it may be Indian," meaning North American Indian, and it developed from there. Maybe this had no bearing on Ellen, who was in a kind of trance, but it could have. On the other hand . . .

A week later I was attending an international heritage conference sponsored by ICOMOS in Ottawa. Normally it focused on architectural heritage, but this time, for the first time, included native sacred sites on its agenda. Walking down a hallway on my way to hear a presentation I passed a native person, our eyes connected, and we both stopped and began to talk. We kept on talking over a cup of tea for a couple of hours. His name was Kenneth Eaglespeaker, a Blackfoot from Alberta and director of Head–Smashed–in–Buffalo–Jump in southern Alberta. He had been sent as a delegate by his employer but had been consigned to the periphery of the conference by the organisers. By contrast, and probably because I was a Professor, I was presenting a paper on the concept of sacred sites and occupied a seat on the closing panel. He was perplexed that the organisation should make such a show about including Native issues before the conference and then basically ignore them during the conference. Then and there I decided to give up my seat on the panel to him and work with the people who had invited me to get him elected to the executive of ICOMOS at the end of the conference. It worked and he succeeded in highlighting native heritage and its preservation as a major ICOMOS concern. The next summer I drove from Regina Saskatchewan to Head–Smashed–In with a friend of mine, Doug Daniels, and I did indeed look out over the plain from the top of the ridge that is the jump itself. The thing about this is that I attended the conference and met Kenneth before I received the notes of Ellen's reading.

Going by the description, the woman with the scholar's hat was definitely not my wife. Though she did get her B.A. many years ago, she was currently working toward an M.A., something she had not been able to do in her years with me. I know that the absence of a career had always bothered her and that I was in some way responsible for the situation. My mother, though, is diminutive and now getting plump, and she always regretted never having had a career during the time she was with my father.

The volume? There was Iain's book, the one I was writing for him—*Return to Eden*. Shortly after he died I decided to scrap it, burn it. But I had given a copy to Don Wiebe at Trinity College, the editor of the series in which it was to have been published. He refused to give me back his copy. I could do what I wanted with my own. "In time, you'll change your mind," he told me. It took some time, but eventually I did. There was also a draft of another book, a reading of Christian Scriptures based on my revelation on the train. I had put this one away too for fear of ridicule, although I did publish a small book interpreting only the Book of Genesis (*Life Before Genesis*, New York: Peter Lang, 1985). As for the "garbage spat at him," there has certainly been plenty of that from "colleagues" in academia who fear the indigenous vision and where I have taken it as a threat to their theoretical security.

Then there was the large tree with falling leaves, the maple at the end of the lane again? And, again, the significance of a fir tree.

I put an eye in the bird when Kate sent it back—where I thought it ought to go. The bird he made for me couldn't see, just as he couldn't see. Now it could.

*   *   *   *

Whether you believe Ellen really was in touch with Iain or not, and my own doubts began to creep back in during the months that followed, you cannot fail but be moved by the compassion that reached across the ocean to help someone who, in Ellen's case, was a complete stranger.

I wrote to Ellen thanking her for her reading and received the following reply dated December 2:

Dear David,

    Thank you for your letter. I will pass it on to Kate today as I have other things to post to her, to help her in the work she has ahead of her with my people.

Before I go on David, I must assure you that the Spiritual messages and work that I do goes no further then the person in need of help. As in your case, Kate who was here to do the writing and because of your friendship. I am a mere vessel for those in the "Spirit" world who chose to use me and once I have passed the message on, I have no idea what has been said, for that reason I like people to write it down, so we can discuss it later to make everything clear. And the person needing help isn't disturbed in any way.

There are times that I get blown away with the proof of what is received at times, as with a tree that came through for you (as I'm writing this I have lots of "white" Spirits Lights around for you, so beautiful). Back to the tree. Kate and I went to the University of Waikato while she was here & there in the grounds was your tree (photo 7). We have taken photos for you.

10:15 a.m.–10:29 a.m. Have 4 elderly dark gentlemen here for you—they say Walk Tall and be Proud—much work ahead for you—they sit in a square within a circle—you will return to the Fair Lady to complete the work you began where the Sun sinks into the Indian Ocean and flowers bloom in the Spring. [The writing begins to scrawl off the bottom of the page and then stops.]

We leave you now in the Light of our love,

Good morning.

I began my work with the Aborigines in Perth, West Australia, where the sun does indeed set into the Indian Ocean. However, return to the Fair Lady to complete my work? In connection with my work with the Aborigines, I had no idea what this might mean.

Folded in Ellen's letter was another piece of paper with another message. It had come to her at 9:20 a.m. on December 1st.

Was thinking about you at above time & a lovely voice, with laughter in, said "Tell him I will be back to see him again." and as I'm writing have been shown a very light white bird like a heron. Very beautiful.

David you have proof of your son, he is safe & will help you whenever your need is great. I must go now. But will be in touch again.

Love & thoughts,

P.S. Please feel free to ask me for help any time.

I thought I had let Iain go. He would not come back. I was better now . . . .

The night of December 4th I had a dream. I am looking for someone. Two other people are with me. I don't know who they are or whom we are looking for. There is a dark passageway, and we have to go into it. I set off in the darkness and then lose sight of the other two. Now I am all by myself and afraid. Suddenly a hand grips mine. The touch is so real I think I must be awake. I am.

I think to myself that I must have been looking for Iain. However, it wasn't Iain's grip. It was an older person's. Two friends of mine had died recently. One was Professor John Holmes of Trinity College who had unsuccessfully tried to contact me in Darwin the previous summer to tell me he had cancer and was about to die. The other was old Joe Mackler, a neighbour of ours in North Burgess Township. At first glance he appeared a crotchety old bachelor, but he really was a dear sweet man who became very close to Iain when he was sick. The two of them used to go hand in hand for long walks together. He was devastated by Iain's death. He too had died recently. The moment I thought of Joe I knew it was his grip.

Another letter dated December 13th arrived from Ellen, along with some photos and a framed message—the one Kate had written down from the Indian during the second reading. In this letter she said "it would be nice to meet you one day. If you're this way at any time please feel free to call, there will be a bed for you." I wrote back that I was indeed planning to return to Australia in the (Canadian) summer of 1989 and that I would come via New Zealand where I had relatives, and visit her. I had decided to continue with my work with the Aborigines and revisit Groote Eylandt.

Then in late February, with me back to work and the events of the readings quickly receding from my mind, I received an unexpected letter from Ellen dated January 6th.

> Dear David,
> I would love to have you call into N.Z. on your way to Aust. We could spend many hours talking. When you come, please bring your reading with you & and we can discuss anything that you don't understand. I never remember the messages that come through me, as I'm a mere vessel for those in the "Spirit" world.

This part of the letter ended abruptly and was followed by another one written much later:

Dear David,

As you can see I started to write to you on the 6th, now it's the end of the month.

I would like to invite you to stay with us while in N.Z. There are a few very Special People I would like you to meet. Look forward to hearing from you soon.

Received 12:15 a.m., 31-1-89: Trimmed your beard & bought a new light blue jersey. New hankies with D on. Not used. Still in gift wrapping. A willow tree without leaves, branches touching the water.

David, this came through from "Spirit" as I was writing to you. Very clear from two lovely boys. Lots of Light around.

Be of good cheer, you are not alone,

This message made me sit up and take notice. That very day, January the 30th in Canada, my daughter Michelle had come to Perth for a visit. She had commented on my scruffy appearance the last time I had seen her, and I had made a point of trimming my beard and brushing my hair before she arrived. Almost the first thing she said to me when I saw her was, "Dad, you need a new sweater," and she had taken me out to look for one. This is the one and only time she'd ever done anything like this. It was her way of buying me a present (with, of course, my money). It was a very special day for both of us. After making the rounds of the stores downtown she eventually chose one at Shaw's, sort of blue-green in colour, and I have treasured it ever since.

New hankies? No. But there were my dad's which my mother had given me, and I had not used them.

The willow tree? Well, there was a willow tree and it was connected with Bryan, my other boy. It stood to the right of our cottage on Otty Lake where we lived when he died. It was on the waterfront and its leaves reached down into the water. All just a coincidence? If so, there were getting to be a lot of them.

I never did make it to New Zealand that year. Nor to Australia for that matter. That was because of what happened next.

4

NOTRE DAME DU CALVAIRE

I remember the third and last time I saw Iain after he died. It was at the Cistercian monastery of Notre Dame du Calvaire in Rogersville New Brunswick in May of 1989.

*　　*　　*　　*

Despite the release I had experienced in my apartment at Trinity that night and what followed from Ellen's readings, I had not made much progress. Even a year after Iain's death I was just barely hanging on. Something was still wrong. I had continued teaching my classes at the University but without a sense of purpose. Then I met John Lokko (photo 9), a Catholic priest from Ghana who was here studying anthropology and enrolled in my graduate course. His aim was to come to a better understanding of his Catholicism in relation to his people's traditional religion. During the 1988/89 academic year we became good friends and often discussed my loss. By the end of term I was really stressed out, and John sensed my plight. He invited me to accompany him on a retreat to a Trappist monastery in New Brunswick along with his fellow–countryman and friend Francis Cujoe the vicar of Notre Dame de Grace church in Moncton. It didn't matter that I wasn't Catholic. The monks would welcome me anyway.

We arrived in Moncton on the 16th and spent the night at Notre Dame de Grace. Having the two of them together was infectious. They never stopped talking and laughing. It was an ability to live in the moment—something I seemed to lack.

Wednesday May 17th was a good morning to be driving to Rogersville. Seventy degrees (lower 20s C) and sunny, and my spirits were high. The car was filled with the sounds of laughter and African music as we rolled along Highway 126 north out of Moncton. The rock and water, pine and spruce, a clearing and a farm house here and there—all were familiar territory to someone from the Ottawa Valley. As John and Francis reminisced about home I gazed out the window wondering what lay ahead. I anticipated containment and silence at the monastery, to have no distractions, to be filled with nothing more than the sound of silence and music. The Trappists are bound to a vow of silence except when they chant the psalms during their offices or common worship. I had always led with my mind rather than my heart or whatever we call those feelings there. Always the intellectual, always analysing and criticising. Perhaps in silence I would learn how to stop.

As we continued on, the landscape started to drift by without my noticing it. Then, abruptly, we were there. It was about 4 o'clock. "Notre Dame du Calvaire," the sign said (photo 10). We turned off the highway and on to a long driveway leading to a brick building that I thought must be the monastery. On my left were freshly ploughed fields, in the air the smell of soil and spruce. On the right, just below us through the trees was a stream and, upstream, a small waterfall. Beyond that, what looked like a lake. As we approached the brick building I noticed that there were actually two, an older one to the right and a newer one just before us. I thought this must be the guest quarters. Behind the larger building were a silo and barn. The monks, I understood, ran a dairy farm. To the left again was what looked like a large chicken coop. Men in overalls and boots seemed to be cleaning it out. Beyond all this again, more ploughed fields.

Francis, it turns out, wasn't to stay with us after all. He was going to return to Moncton to resume his duties. It was to be just John and I. We entered the guest house and proceeded to the front desk. Maybe it was my state of mind, because it couldn't really have meant anything at all, but the monk at the front desk was Father Roger—in Rogersville. My younger brother was named Roger and he died. I passed on the name to my Aboriginal friend Gula's child on Groote Eylandt in Australia (photo 35) and he died. It was Iain's middle name and he died. I couldn't help myself. As soon as Francis departed and John went off to meet another monk I poured out my soul to Roger, a complete stranger. The hope for containment and silence all gone in an instant. Did I still need release? That much? Roger's response was to listen and then tell me his own story. He had come to Calvaire on retreat 13 years ago, much as I was doing now, suffering not so much from loss as aimlessness. He had been Anglican and he'd proceeded through meditation, eastern religions, sex, drugs, and rock and roll, but without finding himself. Here he had found his calling and stayed.

*   *   *   *

I had read up on the Trappists, in particular the Trappists of Rogersville, before I came. An article on them had appeared in the May 1989 issue of *Saturday Night*, and John had given it to me. The Trappist Order can be traced back to the seventeenth century when Don Armand Jean Le Bouthillier de Rance established "the Independent Order of Cistercians of Strict Observance" at La Trappe in Normandy, France. The Observance in question was the *Rule*, a handbook for monastic contemplation, written by St. Benedict, a sixth century Roman hermit (b. 480 d. 547). The Cistercians had emerged as a reform movement aimed at re–establishing the letter of Benedict's *Rule* at the turn of the twelfth century. At the time the monasteries had become wealthy and worldly, more concerned with political power than quiet contemplation.

The Benedictine form of Christian asceticism—the austere and abstemious life—differed from its predecessor in that it shifted the contemplator inside the walls of a monastery and isolated the monastery from the outside world. For 200 years prior to this the contemplative lived out his or her life as a hermit or even within a normal family life.

Benedict sought to enforce contemplation by placing a prohibition on unnecessary speech. The only necessary speech was considered to be the orders given by the master to his disciples. This rule of silence came to define the Trappist way of life.

Until Vatican II the Trappists uttered virtually no words at all. Apart from the master or abbot and his orders, chanting during the Divine Offices was virtually their sole means of verbal expression. As Shapiro says in his *Saturday Night* article, "the monks held their tongues, doing everything together but wordlessly, moving through their days in a kind of mute lock step." Monks might work and pray together for years, eat at the same table, exchange smiles and glances, but never know where each other came from or why they had come. What did develop instead of words, however, was an elaborate system of signs. Communication found a way.

The lifestyle of the early Trappists was abstemious to say the least. On entering the monastery the monks renounced all material possessions. They slept on the floor on straw mats and moved "cowed and bent–headed" through the cloisters dressed in habits and underclothes of coarse sacking. They rose before dawn and divided their day between chanting, contemplation, manual labour and meals. Their meals consisted of boiled vegetables and bread. Infractions of the *Rule* were duly noted and proclaimed to all in the Chapter of Faults where a suitably humiliating penance was prescribed.

In 1967 the rules were revised more to reflect the spirit rather than the letter of Benedict's *Rule*. Speech in the form of brief conversations was now to be allowed without having to seek permission and The Chapter of Faults was abolished. Silence, though, was still the rule in chapel, refectory and chapter. Surprisingly, at least to observers who assumed that silence was psychologically repressive, not much changed after the rules were relaxed. As Shapiro observes, the monks, it seems, found they had not much to say to each other after all. But more to the point, permission to speak did not alter the monks' main reason for being there. That was to harness silence to the task of finding God.

Silence did cause grief, particularly in times of loneliness and doubt, but, on the other hand, it also provided a necessary space between people living at very close quarters day after day, year after year.

The first word of Benedict's *Rule* is "Listen": listen carefully to the master's instructions, listen and open your eyes to the light that comes from God and open your ears to the voice from heaven.

Day 1: Vespers

I was shown to my room on the second floor. It was simple and, of course, immaculate. The window faced south and overlooked the laneway that lead into the monastery. A chair sat beside the window, a setting inviting reading and reflection. A Catholic Bible rested on the bureau. I unpacked my bag, took out my own New King James Version, and placed it on the table beside the bureau. I washed my hands and face in the sink in the far corner of the room and then returned downstairs intending to walk around the grounds before attending Vespers in the chapel at 5:25 p.m. Outside, I turned left toward the lake and walked around to the side of the monastery building itself. A steel gate led to the farmyard and the barn beyond. I unclasped the chain, opened the gate, and walked through, being careful to close the gate and reclasp the chain behind me. As I glanced back over the fence to the courtyard I noticed a man dressed in overalls coming toward me from the small cottage on the left. Politely he informed me that I was not allowed in the farmyard without special permission. Equally politely I apologised for my mistake and returned through the gate.

Back inside, I located the entrance to the main chapel at the eastern end of the guest wing. The chapel itself was in the monastery proper. The point of transition between the two buildings was marked by a small shrine of flickering candles. I lit one for Iain. The chapel itself was square–cut and simple, the atmosphere silent and holy. The windows faced east, anticipating the morning sun. A painting of the sun's rays shone up from the altar to "illuminate" a crucified Jesus. Two rays to the right "fell" on the Virgin Mary.

I seated myself on a pew on the left, second row from the back, trying as much as possible to remain inconspicuous. First off, I'm not Catholic and, second, I was ignorant of the order of service. Then I knelt down on the floor forgetting all about the kneeler up under the pew in front of me. My foot reached back under the pew behind me and hit the kneeler hidden there, knocking it down with a resounding "bang." Oh God! At that moment I felt like crawling under my seat! In the chapel especially, silence is golden. At least the monks had not yet entered. At precisely 5:30 the monks filed in, garbed in their white robes. One man was in street clothes. I assumed he must be a novice. Each entered, stood for a moment, bowed to the Tabernacle, crossed himself, and moved to his stall. I counted 18 in all. The service lasted half–an–hour. It consisted mainly of Plain Song or chant and it was entirely in French. Shapiro describes it beautifully:

> Seigneur, ouver mes lèvres; et ma bouche publiera ta louange. The chant is simple, but more melodic than its Gregorian grandfather. The gentle French vowels and rolling consonants wash through the night, the low voices in near–perfect unison, pausing in the middle of every verse, hitting the next note together every time. Every few minutes, the monks swish forward and their psalter pages flutter, but the singers know their lines, know these psalms that have been sung since long before Christ was born. And after each, the little hymn of praise to the Trinity that is sung dozens of times a day: Gloire au Père, et au Fils, et au Saint–Esprit, au Dieu qui est, qui était, et qui vient, pour les siècles des siècles. Amen.

I knew French but I didn't really understand much of what was happening. But I felt better.

As I was leaving the chapel I ran into one of the monks in the corridor. He thought I was a priest. He had heard two priests were coming in today. I was more than a bit surprised that he talked to me. I had thought that speech was forbidden in this part of the monastery. I corrected him about me being a priest, said good–bye, and went to dinner in the guests' quarters.

Monks and priests ate separately. Our meal consisted of soup, pasta and vegetables. Very basic and very good. It was all prepared on the premises by a cook employed from outside the monastery and delivered to us on a tray by Roger. We served ourselves from here. The monks don't eat meat, but we, as guests, occasionally did. I sat with John, a middle–aged fellow from Toronto who was completing his retreat, and an Acadian "French–Canadian" who didn't speak any French. After dinner I went back to my room. I didn't know why, but the stress was returning. It was all in the back of my neck and shoulders. I went for a walk. Why couldn't I relax? I was suddenly self–conscious of carrying my camera. Always the observer. Or maybe it was the strain of operating almost entirely in French. I needed release. There was still a lot bottled up inside. But why?

At 8 p.m. I attended the final Office of the day, Compline. This time, no banging about in the chapel. I counted 21 monks, two in street clothes. Afterwards I returned to my room and glanced at the booklet I bought downstairs called *La Vie Monastique Chez les Cisterciens–Trappistes de Rogersville*. It opened with a quote from Vatican II (Gaudium et spes, N. 57):

> Lorsqu' il cultive la terre de ses mains ou avec l'aide de moyens technique pour qu'elle produise des fruits et devienne une demeure digne de toute la famille humaine, et lorsqu' il prend part conscienment à la vie des groupes sociaux, l'homme réalise le plan de Dieu . . .

In productive labour one discovers one's humanity and God's plan. The monks here certainly laboured on their farm, and I thought that some hard labour might do me a lot of good right then. I decided to ask if I could help out. Other quotations in the booklet struck my eye. The first were from Matthew 19:

16: And behold, one came up to him saying, "teacher, what good deed must I do, to have eternal life?"

17: And He said to him, "Why do you ask me about what is good? One there is who is good. If you would enter life, keep the commandments."

18: He said to him, "Which? And Jesus said. "You shall not kill. You shall not commit adultery. You shall not steal, You shall not bear false witness,

19: Honour your father and mother, and, you shall love your neighbour as yourself."

20: The young man said to him, "All these I have observed; What do I still lack?"

21: Jesus said to him, "If you would be perfect, go, sell what you possess and give to the poor, and you will have treasure in heaven; and come, follow me."

22: However, Jesus failed to convince the young man in question; instead the young man went away disappointed, his wealth being great.

23: And Jesus said to his disciples, "Truly, I say to you, it will be hard for a rich man to enter the kingdom of heaven."

24: "And again I tell you, it is easier for a camel to go through the eye of a needle than for a rich man to enter the kingdom of God."

25: When his disciples heard this they were greatly astonished, saying, "Who then can be saved?"

26: But Jesus looked at them and said to them, "With men this is impossible, but with God all things are possible."

27: Then Peter said in reply, "Lo, we have left everything and followed you. What then shall we have?"

28: Jesus said to them, "Truly I say to you, that in the new world, when the Son of Man shall sit on his glorious throne, you who have followed me will also sit on twelve thrones, judging the twelve tribes of Israel.

29: And every one who has left houses or brothers or sisters or father or mother or children or lands, for My name's sake, will receive a hundredfold, and inherit eternal life.

30: But many that are first will be last, and the last first."

The Trappists of Rogersville seemed to embody all of what Matthew is saying here. They are men and women (at the Trappistine monastery nearby) who have renounced material possessions, replaced ties of kinship and family with ties to God and who, in their day–to–day living, do not beg but produce mainly for others and not to make a profit but merely to maintain themselves.

I read on about the history of the monastery. Notre Dame du Calvaire was founded in 1902 by six monks from the Abbey of

Bonnecombe in the Diocese of Rodez in France. They had come seeking a more favourable setting in which to practice their vocation, the French government being somewhat unsympathetic to the monastic practice at the time. They approached the Curé of Rogersville, Marcel–François Richard, who was able to provide them with land and assist them settling in. In the spring of 1904 these six were joined in a separate establishment by a group of Cistercinenes–Trappistines de Vaise—nuns—from the diocese of Lyon in France.

Today the farm provides the monks with their means of livelihood. Tasks are diversified not in the interests of economic efficiency but in order "to permit each monk to respond to the exigencies of his temperament." There are outside tasks involving farming and forestry and inside tasks such as cooking, laundry, and housekeeping. Monks are permitted to change tasks as their "temperament" changes, moving between the outside and the inside.

The Trappists' day is divided between prayer (seven hours), study (five hours), and manual labour (six hours), as set down by St. Benedict in the *Rule*. The aim of the routine is to create a balance, to satisfy the whole person. The remaining hours are for eating and sleeping. Study is mainly focused on the Bible, but a monk may also pursue philosophy, science, or music.

> Seven times a day I praise thee,
> for of thy righteous ordinances.
>
> (Psalm 119: 164)

Seven times a day they do indeed pray. Services involve psalmody, scripture readings, hymns, anti–phones, and responses. The order of daily services—the Divine Office—is outlined by St. Benedict in the *Rule*:

The day begins where it ends, with Night Office or Vigil. The last nocturne of Vigil begins at 4:15 a.m. and lasts for 45 minutes. This is followed by a half hour of private prayer followed by breakfast. At 6:30 the monks are called to Laude and at 7:45 to Tierce. At 8 a.m. is Concelebrated Mass, the mid–point in the daily prayer journey. After Mass, at 9 a.m., the monks leave for work. At 11:40 they are recalled to Sext. Dinner, the main meal of the day, is at 12 noon. After a period of rest, at 2 p.m. the monks proceed to None (the 9th hour of Jesus' death on the cross) for 10 minutes and then return to work. At

5:25 they are called to Vespers. Supper follows at 6 p.m., Compline at 8 p.m., just before bedtime. The first nocturne of Night Office commences at midnight.

What a routine it was. I was tired just reading this.

It was now well past 10, and I wanted to be up for Night Offices tomorrow morning. I was determined to follow the monks' schedule. After all, wasn't this what I was here for? To participate in something outside myself?

Day 2: Compline

I woke to my alarm at 3:45 a.m. My eyes felt heavy, my face drawn. It was more than just being stressed out. There was a rawness inside me, about the heart. It was like someone scraping out the insides of my chest with a clam shell.

Four a.m. Time to go to Night Offices.

After the service I returned to my room. It was no use trying to go back to sleep. I picked up the Revised Standard Catholic Bible and leafed randomly through the pages.

> Mark 10: 23–24 And Jesus looked around and said to his disciples, "How hard it will be for those who have riches to enter the kingdom of God!" And the disciples were amazed at his words. But Jesus said to them again, "Children, how hard it is to enter the kingdom of God!"

This followed along the same lines as the first passage I had turned to. Is it being rich that's the problem or what you have to do to get rich?—the greed and competition that exploits and harms other people.

I came to Luke 21: 23–28:

> "For great distress shall be upon the earth and wrath upon this people; they will fall by the edge of the sword, and be led captive among all nations; and Jerusalem will be trodden down by the Gentiles, until the times of the Gentiles are fulfilled. And there will be signs in sun and moon and stars, and upon the earth distress of nations in perplexity at the roaring of the sea and the waves, men fainting with fear and foreboding of what is coming on the world; for the powers of heaven will be shaken. And they will see the Son of man coming in a cloud with power and great glory. Now when these things begin to take place, look up and raise your heads, because your redemption is drawing near."

All this misery seemed to me the consequence of the greed and competition I read of in the first passage.

I came to Acts 4: 32, 35:

> Now the company of those who believed were of one heart and one soul, and no one said any of these things which he possessed was his own, but they had everything in common . . . and distribution was made to each as any had need.

This seemed to me an alternative to greed and competition. However, it was not renunciation in the Aboriginal sense where property is held, not in common, but each with his or her own for the purpose of giving it up to someone who has none of it. Was this "oneness" and "commonality" Jesus' teaching, or was it that of his followers after his death?

I move on to Acts 20: 32–35:

> "And now I [Paul] commend you to God and to the word of his grace, which is able to build you up and to give you the inheritance among all those who are sanctified. I coveted no one's silver or gold or apparel. Yes, you yourselves know that these hands ministered to my necessities, and to those who were with me. In all things I have shown you that by so toiling one must help the weak, remembering the words of the Lord Jesus, how he said, 'It is more blessed to give than to receive.'"

This seemed closer to Aboriginal renunciation. By giving to those who have little or nothing the consequence is that they will not be moved to want more themselves, nor be moved to take it away from others.

Then I came upon Romans 8:9:

> But you are not in the flesh, you are in the Spirit, if in fact the Spirit of God dwells in you. Any one who does not have the Spirit of Christ, does not belong to him. But if Christ is in you, although your bodies are dead because of sin, your spirits are alive because of righteousness. If the Spirit of him who raised Jesus from the dead dwells in you, he who raised Christ Jesus from the dead will give life to your mortal bodies also through his Spirit which dwells in you.

That is, if the spirit (of Jesus, of God) is in you, you will be moved to act in a righteous (giving, loving) way. This is rather like what my revelation—what the Aborigines—were telling me, though I did not really understand what they meant.

My reading was interrupted by the call to breakfast.

At 8 o'clock Mass John was invited to celebrate with the monks in the chapel. This was my first day at Mass and I was unsure what to do. I was not Catholic and I knew the church frowned on non-Catholics taking communion. However, I was baptised Anglican which is pretty close to Catholic, and I had been attending a variety of Christian churches off and on over the years. If I was to participate authentically in the monastic experience I should include Mass as well. So I moved out of my pew and stood at the back of the line that was forming to move toward the abbot who was standing at the railing which separated the monk's enclosure from the congregation as he prepared to offer the bread. As I moved forward to take my turn, I thought to myself, "Let him know you're not Catholic so he can make the choice whether or not to give you communion." I was next. I panicked. I looked at the abbot as he was about to give me a wafer and said, "Je suis Anglican." He glanced with me with a puzzled look on his face and responded "Quoi?" I realised I'd blown it. Speech was absolutely forbidden in the chapel and now I'd got *him* talking. But I repeated myself anyway,

"Suis Anglican."

This time a small smile of understanding emerged on his lips. He nodded his head, took the wafer and popped it straight into my open mouth, ignoring my cupped hands down near my chest. I swallowed the wafer, rose and returned to my pew, red as a beet from embarrassment. The ordeal, the Mass, over, I returned to my room.

The stress in my neck had subsided somewhat, but I was very tired and it was only 9 a.m. I glanced out the window. It was another beautiful day. I resisted the temptation to go back to bed and instead went downstairs to tell Brother Leo I wanted to work while I was here—any kind of work they wanted. He asked what experience I had and I told him I'd owned a small farm. So he told me I could work in the barn with Father Maurice. First, though, I would need boots and overalls, and these he got from the store room. At the barn, Maurice suggested I start by cleaning out the stalls, i.e., shovel manure. I did, loading it into bins and pulling them outside. After some time Maurice asked me to go up into the loft and move some bales of hay from one end of the floor to the chutes in the middle where they could be dropped downstairs for the cattle.

The bales and some loose hay were piled right up to the window. This was going to be a big job. I started loading the bales on a trolley, one by one. However, just when I had three tiers loaded they began to sway and they all fell off. So I tried again. Same result, but at least they waited until I started pulling the trolley. This was ridiculous. I'd done this kind of work all the time and never had this happen. Then I began to see the humour in my situation and started laughing. I was all thumbs and just not thinking straight. I'd been this way for a long time. Right: "Stack the bales side by side on the trolley first on the bottom, then end to end a layer above, then side by side again above that." Finally I had it working and got into a rhythm, forgetting all about going to Sext at 11:40. However, I did hear the bell for lunch.

I was hot and tired and full after lunch so I went for a walk outside by the dam and the grotto (photo 11). I sat above it on the steps and gazed at the waterfall. The sun was warm on my face and I began to doze. Suddenly I woke with a start. To my right, coming up the steps toward me was someone who looked like a latter–day Moses. Long white hair, a beard, dressed in brown robes, staff in hand.

"You must be Brother Anthony," I blurted out as he reached me, guessing he was the hermit who, I was told, lived in a cabin on the other side of the grotto.

"Yes," came back the reply. "And you must be David Turner. I knew you were coming."

Then he peered at me, leaned forward, his eyes meeting mine and said,

"Haven't we met before? Weren't you at Carleton University? Let's see. In the mid–'60s?"

I had been and the more I looked at him the more familiar he seemed. He had been a doctor and had given it up to be a monk. He had been at Carleton University in Ottawa while I was doing my B.A. I think I had met him at St. Patrick's College.

"That's amazing," I said. "How could you remember someone from a brief meeting so long ago?"

He smiled and looked at me reassuringly, "Oh," he says, "I don't get to meet all that many people."

He knew I was coming from Francis Cujoe. He said he wanted to talk to me at length while I was here, a strange request from a hermit at a Trappist monastery! He told me he had written a book on Old Testament precedents in the New Testament. It was for sale in the monastery gift shop. When I returned to the guest quarters after our conversation I bought a copy. It was called *The Bread of God* "by a monk who prayed for a hermit who wrote." While Anthony researched and wrote, another hermit, Brother Donald, sat in his own cabin across the lake and prayed for his success. Anthony's calling was to convert the Jews. Leafing through the book, I thought: if you could demonstrate enough Old Testament precedents for the New Testament, mightn't Christians just as readily be converted to Judaism?

After attending None I returned to my work in the barn.

Next I was asked to clean out the silo. This was where feed was stored. I loaded the silage into a bin and pulled it backwards down the narrow walkway between the cattle where I was supposed to dump it out. I suddenly realised I'd done something stupid. I would have to empty it out in front of me then push the bin back over the pile of silage in order to get back to the silo. Boy, I thought, am I going to look silly. So I prayed no one was watching and pushed. Just as I managed to get the bin about half way up over the pile I glanced over to the other side of the stalls to see this old wizened monk standing there looking at me with a very puzzled look on his face. I laughed to myself at myself. The monk must have sensed my predicament because he just smiled back and went on his way. I finished my job and I walked down to the other end of the barn to see what Leo was doing. We talked.

Leo is a lay monk, he's not a priest like Roger and Maurice. He's been here for 35 years. Leo can barely read or write—just enough to get by but not enough to engage in serious study. He used to run the farm but that job's been taken over by Maurice who has been schooled in modern farming techniques such as, says Leo, knowing not to feed the cows silage before milking because it puts an unpleasant taste in the milk. Leo tells me of two brothers who came from the States to become monks. They knew no French but are now almost fluent. Their gift is singing so that's what they do. His is physical labour, and he certainly looks the part. He reminds me of another Leo, Leo Boivan, a French–Canadian hockey player who played for the Boston Bruins some years ago. Leo tells me what he likes about life at the monastery: you don't work too much, you don't pray too much, and you don't study too much, not to mention eat too much! Brother Anthony, Leo says, is not a Trappist but a third degree Carmelite.

It was 5:25 and I was off to Vespers. It occurred to me that by singing the same Psalms again and again, day after day, month after month, year after year, the words must mean less and less to the singers and the form of the music become more and more apparent. Does the melodic line of the music *embed* itself in each monk to replace the content of his self, his personality? Is this part of the process of "emptying" oneself to make one's self receptive to "God" or whatever else is "out there?"

I put my insight to Roger. "Perhaps," he said, "but don't forget that the Psalms are also the word of God." To a Trappist the word and their meanings are more significant than the forms within which they are expressed. But maybe that's not the way it actually works in practice.

After supper I was sitting in my room by the window overlooking the laneway (photo 12). when I heard someone coming down the hall. My door was open; it was the abbot, Dom Alphonse. He was coming to apologise *to me* for not understanding what I was trying to tell him at Mass that morning. And here I should have gone and apologised to him for disturbing his service.

"Just what were you trying to tell me," he asked gravely.

That I wasn't Catholic and shouldn't be taking communion, I replied.

A big smile of relief spread on his face. "Well, normally we have to ask the Bishop's permission," he said, "but in your case we'll make an exception." I could relax.

Later that evening I went to the library and, scanning the shelves for something to read, came across Thomas Merton's *The Waters of Siloe* on the history of the Trappists. Thomas Merton is probably the most famous of the Trappists, largely because of his literary talents and his spiritual outreach to other branches of Christianity and the world religions.

Thomas Merton was born in 1915 in the French Pyrénées of a New Zealand father and an American Quaker mother, an auspicious beginning to say the least. He was raised in rural Long Island and in Douglastown, New York, with sojourns in Bermuda, France, and England. His mother died from cancer when he was six, and in 1931 his father died of a brain tumour. Thereafter he remained in England with his godfather. An academic career at Cambridge in England and Columbia University in New York followed during which time he became a card–carrying communist. However, in 1937 he converted to Catholicism having been heavily influenced by his reading of Christian mysticism. His M.A. thesis was on William Blake. After a brief and unsuccessful stint with the Franciscans, Merton entered the Trappist monastery at Gethsemane, Kentucky in 1941 at the age of 27. He was to remain there for 27 years and, in fact, died on the date marking the anniversary of his entry into the monastery. In 1947 he took his vows as a monk and, in 1949, as a priest. From 1965 until his death he lived as a hermit attached to the monastery. It was during this period that he visited Asia to pursue his interest in Christian and Eastern mysticism. Among the 60 books he wrote in his lifetime are *The Asian Journal of Thomas Merton* (1973), *Zen and the Birds of Appetite* (1968), *Gandhi on Non–violence* (1965), *Seeds of Contemplation* (1949), *The Waters of Siloe* (1949), and *The Seven Story Mountain* (1948).

Day 3: Night Office

I woke up at 3:45 to my alarm, determined to make it to Night Office. I had a headache and was slightly nauseous. I sat through the service dulled to what was being enacted before me. As I returned to my room, it felt like my feet were stuck in cement. I still had a headache. What was wrong? Despite my wish to, I didn't seem to be emptying myself at all. If anything, I was feeling worse than when I arrived.

After breakfast I headed out to the barn to continue moving hay. However, before I climbed up into the loft I stopped to talk to Maurice. He knew something of my loss from Roger and he said he understood. He had lost both his parents and all his siblings to cancer and had leukaemia himself. Fortunately, it was now in remission. No matter how bad things get, I thought, there's always someone who has it much worse than you do. I climbed up into the loft still with a headache and again feeling nauseous. Then I climbed to the top of the bales and loose hay piled at the end of the barn and sat down. My thoughts turned to Iain and I began to cry. It all poured out. Then I threw up. Eventually the spasms subsided so I cleaned up and slid down the hay and started back to work, my headache and the nausea finally gone.

I loaded up my bales and trolleyed them over to the chute. One of them fell off. As I bent to pick it up I was aware of someone in the loft. I looked up with a start and called out "Iain" as my eye picked up a presence in front of me and followed it toward the southern end of the barn where the stacks were. It was sort of oblong in shape and translucent, as in my previous two experiences, and about two feet off the ground. There were no features but I knew it was Iain. He vanished as my eye continued on, up the bales to the window. There was a swallow on the top of the lower frame banging against the glass, trying to get out. My glance turned left toward the other window and there was another swallow with the same intent.

Almost reflexively I climbed the pile of bales to the window on my right. As I approached it the swallow became calm and I lifted up the bottom panel of the window intending that the bird should fly out. But the bird's wing caught between the upper and lower frames. It cried in pain or from fright. I stopped what I was doing and reached out and gently pulled the wing free with my hand. The swallow remained motionless in my palm. Then, with my other hand, I finished opening the window and released the swallow and watched as it flew away. Then I turned and walked over to the other window. The swallow was still there, but now sitting motionless on the frame. I picked it up, opened the window, and released it.

Iain had returned as he said through Ellen he would. There were two birds. Two sons.

I must admit that even after my experience in my room at Trinity, even with Ellen's readings, doubt had begun to creep back in. Was it just my mind playing tricks on me? Were the other things coincidences? But, now, after what had just happened in the barn, any doubts I had were dispelled.

The spirit lives. It sustains us in life. It transcends death.

I now knew what that Spiritual Substance was that the Aborigines talked about. I knew because I had sensed it and then seen it, first on the train and now after Iain's death.

*   *   *   *

Life does proceed from "nothingness"—the Nothingness of material-less spiritual substance(s) to which life returns when our material existence ends.

*   *   *   *

After what just happened in the loft I climbed back downstairs to tell Maurice. He listened, reflected for a moment, and said "If you still have any doubts, go back into the loft and try to catch a swallow in your hands." Of course he and I both knew I couldn't.

Day 4: Laud

It was the morning of May 20th. I felt refreshed and eager to begin my day. I hadn't set my alarm and had missed Night Office. But this time it didn't bother me. John had mentioned yesterday that he wanted to go into Moncton today and from there to Fredericton for Francis' graduation party at the University of New Brunswick. Would I go with him? The train left at 6 p.m. I decided to wait until 5 to make up my mind. Meanwhile I would go to Laud and continue the monks' routine. As I worked in the barn I reflected on the events of yesterday, my own state of being, the implications. My mind drifted back to three lectures given by Michael Ignatieff at Trinity College the previous November. The title of the lectures was "All Shook Up" and they were about the shaken-up states of depression, illness and love. Michael was the son of the Provost of Trinity, George Ignatieff, who had welcomed me to the College some years earlier. [What follows here is my recollections edited against the transcripts of these talks now held in the Trinity College Library].

Michael's theme was that our concepts of selfhood stem from the overwhelming importance we attach to personal freedom: self is to be realised in indulgence, in satisfaction in a material sense, in fulfilment in a shallow, personal, way. Social order is to be realised in an unconscious collaboration of individuals, each bent on their own self-interest whose incompatibilities are resolved in the marketplace through the laws of demand and supply [if supply and demand, I reflected, you would take whatever it was the other person had to offer whether you "needed" it or not]. In this world we, as individuals, are brought up unrealistically to believe that we are the masters of our own destiny and that we alone are responsible for our successes and failures. Therefore the terror of failure, illness, ageing and death. Hence depression.

Depression: We have come to think of depression as a chemical imbalance which we can correct by the judicious application of drugs and of psychotherapy. In the mid–nineteenth century the term depression meant "lowness of spirits." Now it means to be virtually incapacitated. The terror of depression is that it mocks our ideas of self–mastery. It is a state in which the self has given up trying. It *must* be curable, else the whole human enterprise as we have defined it, collapses.

Depression, however, is really a grim awakening to the truth which the illusions of normal existence keep hidden. We come to see our former self–confidence as a neurotic delusion. Our will–power, our drive, our ambition, are all nurtured by illusions about ourselves that collapse when we hit the bedrock of our real limitations. In our failure we are taken to the very core of ourselves—to a state of lucidity which casts a cold, grey light on the illusions that sustain us.

Michael put it that there are three types of depression. First is the depression of failure. One has simply given up in the aftermath of failure and to give up is to give up all the causes that made life worth living in the first place. It is the soul's taking stock of the gulf that separates reach from grasp. Second is the depression of success. Having reached the top, one finds one's expectations still unfulfilled. The soul discovers the poverty of the dream itself. The third type of depression has no name. It is simply a certain state of being: despair. All our faith in our capacity to act, will, execute plans, goes into suspension. We desire to escape ourselves while being fixated on ourselves—and we can't [as I had been doing, I reflected]. As we spiral downward, ever downward, into the well of ourselves, we experience a radical rupture with the external world, others, friends, those we love. This ends finally in an absorption in suffering itself, in an obliteration of the *content* of self, a hurt withdrawal from the external world into the private *cell* of the self. Having no self to indulge, we embrace pain as a substitute.

In the speechless twilight, we stare at a mirror which gives back no reflection.

We now enter a mystical state of self–less awareness and recall the primal satisfaction of a life without the dubious and limited pleasures of adult existence. Depression, then, is a tortured meditation on Paradise lost. We can only get out of it—back into the light—not through further introspection, but through the society of others: talking, walking, physical exertion, or as Samuel Johnson observed, "How much happiness is gained, how much misery escaped, by frequent and violent agitation of the body." Now humble and self–effacing, we re–knit ourselves into the fabric of ordinary purpose, ordinary life, in all its redeeming beauty.

But this journey back is really a journey of refilling oneself with all that one had previously emptied out . . . including, sometimes, refilling oneself with what was the source of the problem in the first place. Real redemption surely does not lie in this but in retaining the newly humbled and self–effacing self—that cell of a self—we bring back with us into the so–called "real world."

Illness: Brings us face–to–face with one of the most important ironies in the credo of modern individualism. We think of ourselves as the narrators of our own life's story. Then illness arrives and makes a sorry end of that story. We glorify self–reliance; illness throws us into abject dependence. Modern medicine promises mastery over our bodies; fatal illness shows us the vanity of those wishes.

Stoicism is the ethic of learning to endure without complaint that which we can't mend. In an age of individualism it has come to imply resignation, acceptance of fate. We esteem those who struggle and fight over those who suffer in silence. However, we may be placing unrealistic expectations on ourselves. We may be burdening patients with expectations beyond their capacity to realise. Is it right to add a rack of expectations to an already–existing rack of physical suffering? [In Iain's case we placed the burden of those expectations on ourselves.] Moreover, if the patient is largely responsible for the cure, is he or she then not also responsible for the illness? The implication nags.

In the United States some $247 billion is spent annually on health care, but one third of the patients are not suffering from any treatable disorder. These are individualism's walking wounded: "Why can't I master the world, master others?" It is no coincidence that hypochondria is prevalent among the poor and the homeless. We may take an ironic flight into illness in order to be cared for in unconscious rebellion against a credo that denies the sociability that is the very core of our humanity.

Admittedly, macho stoicism is not a good game to play when up against an illness like cancer. Immunological research does indicate that the body's ability to resist disease can be influenced by psychic states—negatively by stress and anxiety, positively by serenity and determination. The influence of will can explain apparently mysterious remissions from cancer. People who struggle do live longer. Struggle dignifies them in their predicament. We should not abandon the sense of self–responsibility but rather learn to live with it ironically. Struggle, but with the presumption of failure. Accept discomfort, accept fate: There is much that can't be mastered, controlled or understood. Be more tolerant of sadness, depression, melancholy or fear. Be less manic about self–sufficiency, self–promotion and less concerned with self–importance.

Our culture isn't good at dying. The problem with dying is that it makes the whole narrative of selfhood seem senseless, the idea that we are masters of our own lives seem an absurdity. We say we accept death but feel a sense of injustice if it cuts life short. If death is natural, why do we feel that it is unjust? We feel this way because we think we have to write our own life story. However, we don't write the beginning, nor the end, and much of the middle is written by others,

You do not die of being sick, you die of being alive.

Love: May be this civilisation's only remaining project, its ever–receding utopia and its inevitable disappointment, its unstaunchable wound.

Romantic love is market society's cure for the wounds it inflicts. Romantic love is rightly cursed by feminism for consigning women to the enslavement of infatuation and the prison–house of patriarchal marriage. Romantic love celebrates the sovereignty of the desiring self. True love is a revolt against romantic discourse.

The expectations of romantic love are so high that no real marriage can ever measure up to our dreams. Modern divorce rates may reflect the gulf that exists between romantic ideals and marital realities. On a more positive note, individuals are no longer resigned to their fate. They flee, not so much from commitments, as from commitments that smother them.

We must distinguish between what can be changed and what can be endured in a marriage. How does one come to terms with the slow bleaching–away of infatuation? How does one make the transition from passion to endearment?

"Falling in love" is the moment when we exist most transcendentally as individuals. It is, if you will, the Holy Grail of an individualist society. In the mirror of infatuation we see our individuality etched in a transcendent glow. Infatuation is so flattering that we forget that the object of it is really ourselves. People who can't make the passage from infatuation to love can't bear to wake from infatuation and see the "other" for what they really are, warts and all. So they lurch from infatuation to infatuation, victims of romance.

People who do make the passage begin to evaluate the loved one. They begin to see them apart from themselves, see their real outline, their real limits. They learn to love them as they are, not how they wish them to be. No real person comes close to the perfection we glimpse in that first infatuated moment. True love comes when we cease seeing ourselves reflected in the other but see the other as different from ourselves in a way that we can respect. This is to transcend individualism in a different sense. Indeed, it is to dissolve it into relation.

Love, then, is not just a passion but a judgement. Judgement can keep us in love—that respect of another's habits of mind and heart and their whole being in the world. Love, then, is founded on an estimation of a person's character. Judgement can also throw us out of love. We can't stay in love if judgement tells us that the person is without qualities we esteem and admire. More than an extinction of passion, what kills love is moral dissolution.

Love, then, is a difficult enterprise. We want its intimacy but we can't stand its judgement. In the final analysis, we all have the qualities of our defects and the defects of our qualities. If the other is in love with our courage he or she will have to endure our stubbornness; if in love with our energy then he or she will have to live with our compulsiveness. We can't seem to have one without the other. When what we respect in a person is so entwined with what we can't stand about them, we arrive at marriage's hard place.

Eventually, marriage becomes a pitiless encounter with the incorrigible in ourselves and others.

Modern individualism tells us we can change everything. We do not have to endure it. However, we discover in the dreary repetition and compulsion of our worst habits, in the ghastly inability of our spouses to be other than what they are, that human nature is made of very obdurate stuff. Where change becomes all but impossible is when we're asked to alter what we like best about ourselves.

The question "How can I change them?" can rarely be answered in the space of a lifetime. However, you can't endure more than you can stand. Marriages, then, are tests of endurance, forms of forbearance; but our society doesn't value endurance like it used to. It implies resignation, failure to control one's destiny, to be master of one's self.

"Why should I put up with this?" is modernity's basic cry. The answer is, or should be, "Because I love the person in question."

You love them because they're different—different sex, different character, different being, different body. In infatuation you adore these differences; in love you endure them. To insist on the incorrigible otherness of the person you love is to reject the romantic view of love and marriage.

Longing for love in a romantic sense is longing for a secularised form of redemption—to be understood, to be forgiven, to be loved for what we really are. The problem is that we don't always deserve to be loved for what we really are! We ask of our partners a forgiveness they cannot give, for sins and weaknesses that it is not in their power to absolve. Our expectations of these "soulmates" of ours are cruel indeed.

One learns in marriage of the razor–thin line between love and hate. All that inverted pyramid of houses, mortgages, insurance policies, boat houses, boats, islands, children's responsibilities, hangs on this little point, this fragile thread of love or, worse, infatuation.

Is it better for children to endure a loveless marriage in preference to a loveless divorce?

But even in divorce there is this overwhelming need to make retrospective peace with the former partner, to restructure the narrative with at least some form of continuity. The discontinuity of divorce is that the other person was there at the beginning, is there in the middle, but is suddenly not there at the end. It is the person who was supposed to take the place of the parent and the parent is not expected to be there at the end.

The loss of a parent, the loss of a spouse, the loss of a child, is life's rude awakening to the fact that we aren't self-sufficient. Never were.

Love is a shared commitment to give life its meaning, its continuity, its sense over the long haul. With our children we collaborate together to root each other in a dimension of time longer than our own lives. We fear a loveless dying more than death itself. We have a good deal of difficulty enduring death when we think that no one will mourn our going. To be mourned as we go is to feel life coming together into a circle of meaning. The love we received from our parents transmitted intact through our love for each other to our children and their love for us whispered in our ears as we slip into darkness.

Love is not an exchange process. Love will die if people presume that they are loved only to the degree that they satisfy the other. "We do a lot for each other," is the transactional logic not of love but of business. The capacity to sacrifice oneself is the proof that love counts. In a selfish world, who is going to love selflessly without thought to themselves?

*　　*　　*　　*

I thought of Iain who left when he did to save us any more pain, though he was powerless to stop his going. I thought of the love that binds us despite death. I thought of Michelle and how we were drawn together in the circumstances of Iain's leaving, each of us filling in the other the gap which he left. I thought of Graeme and how we remain apart–together trying to find a way back to each other.

*　　*　　*　　*

I decided to go into Moncton with John after all but to return to the monastery when he and Francis left for Fredericton. That afternoon, John and I caught a ride to the train station in Rogersville with one of the lay staff. That evening in Notre Dame de Grace Church in Moncton I took mass from John. Later we went to visit some of Francis' friends, the Bourques, Angèle and Gerry. They were Acadians which translated into straightforward, unassuming, salt–of–the–earth—and a fun time. After a good, hearty meat–and–potatoes dinner and a few glasses of wine, we sat around the living room discussing life at the monastery. The Bourques knew from John why I had gone there and I told them it put things in perspective for me. No matter how bad things are there's always somebody who has it worse, I said, mentioning Maurice. Angèle's brother had been at the monastery as a novice but quit after six months because of what he saw as the over–importance attached to insignificant rules. Like not being allowed to see his nephew when he visited, like not being able to take a shower after work and before prayer, like not being able to get something to eat after work. He said the abbot was very upset when he left and relaxed some of the rules. However, he didn't go back.

Almost imperceptibly the room seemed to empty around Angèle and me. We were left alone and she asked me about Iain. I told her about what happened in the barn at Notre Dame du Calvaire.

"What do you make of it?" I asked.

"I don't question it," she replied. "Something very special has been revealed to you. It happens to very few people. Iain came back to tell you he was safe."

She rose from her chair and walked away, motioning me to stay where I was. Soon she returned with a small box. Opening it, she drew out a small medal of the Virgin Mary. "It is from Medjugorje," she said. "It's very special to me. I want you to have it." Medjugorje is the parish in Yugoslavia where the Virgin Mary appeared to six young people in a series of apparitions dating from June 24, 1981. She first appeared in the indistinct form of a young girl in a grey robe whose face was gently shining. Her message to "a world bent on self–destruction" was "Peace, peace, peace, be reconciled."

Angèle too, like Maurice, said, "Try touching a bird in the barn again. You'll never be able to do it."

There was indeed something sacred about that moment in the barn. For an instant, time stood still, space ceased to be a barrier, and a bridge was crossed.

Day 5: Tierce

The next morning, Sunday, I rose early for mass at Notre Dame de Grace with Francis and John. When the time arrived for communion, this time I was ready. Up I marched in the middle of the procession and eventually found myself face–to–face with the woman administering the rite. She looked at me, hesitated for a moment, then placed a wafer in the outstretched palm of my hand.

Further on in the mass, as the congregation knelt to pray, I wondered if petitioning wasn't a sign of decay in a religion. I mean in the sense of asking someone or some power to do things for you or make things turn out all right. It was that selfishness issue again—thinking of "me first." Instead I tried to put all thought out of my mind and after a few moments I began to feel the silence.

After mass, over a cup of coffee at the rectory, Francis said, "Sister Lefrance [the woman giving communion] came to me after mass and asked me who you were. She says she knows you from somewhere." I told him that I was sure I had never met her, but to make certain I went and talked to her. She was insistent, but wasn't sure where. I'd never been to Moncton and she'd never been to the places I've been. But she was so sure.

That afternoon John and Francis drove me back to Rogersville and the monastery, even though their destination, Fredericton, is in the opposite direction. They had their Ghanaian music and each other's company, and they were happy just to drive. We arrived at Calvaire just in time for supper. Roger was glad to see me and told me that they were wondering if I really was coming back. That evening, after Compline, alone in my room, I relaxed with Thomas Merton's *The Waters of Siloe*. I felt a surge of energy and read well into the night.

Day 6: Concelebrated Mass

I woke on Monday morning, calm and refreshed, but once again too late for Night Office and Laud. However, I did make my way down for Tierce and Concelebrated Mass. The monks filed silently in and took their places. Suddenly I had an impression of robeForms over and above the contents of the robes—the monks—themselves. The chapel seemed to separate down the middle, the Forms on one side appearing to mirror those on the other. It made me think of Jaleh Jam's painting of The Last Supper which hung on the wall of my apartment back home (photo 13). It recalled my experience of "laughing waves" with the Aborigines (page xvi), and of what appeared to be myself sitting down there on the seat in the train while I watched from above. Was this the *awarrawalya* or "outer spirit" the Aborigines spoke of?

Later that evening, after Vespers, I talked to Roger about my robeform experience. He wasn't sure, but he thought he had once experienced something like it one evening at dinner. He was sitting at his table when he looked up at another monk sitting nearby. All at once his face seemed to take on a different quality, almost as if it was like a mask, and he saw something about this monk that was ageless—timeless. The impression vanished when the monk caught sight of his gaze and began to feel uncomfortable. Roger never mentioned to him what had happened. Roger and I talked about this kind of experience as "religious experience." He said he didn't think it was, or at least it wasn't the *kind* of experience he was hoping to have in contemplation as a monk. He was trying to reach God, but he had no idea what that might mean until he did and, as yet he thought he hadn't. "What if what you saw in that monk's face was a reflection of the God you are trying to reach," I asked. My question seemed to agitate him and so I just left it at that.

We talked about interpreting Scriptures. I mentioned my Bible readings to him and how I understood them. Without debating my interpretations he simply said, "Though Christ revealed the fullness of the truth, we are constantly finding out more of what it is." He had a point. No one knows what Jesus really meant. He wrote not a word. All we have are reports after the fact. If what he had to say in his time was really different from what was then commonly known, how could he have been fully understood? This idea reminded me of the story of the Zen Buddhist Master and his American student. Every year the American would come to visit him in Japan to continue his instruction and every year return home to ponder what he had learned. Finally, after 20 years, during one of their sessions, the student suddenly exclaimed, "Master, Master, finally I understand what you have been trying to teach me all of these years."

"Oh," said the Master thoughtfully and with some concern, "then I must not have expressed myself properly."

Now, after six days in the monastery there was music in my heart. I heard, felt, the melodies of the chants whenever I began to get anxious, and the anxiety disappeared.

Day 7: Sext

It was Tuesday, May 23rd. I was in the second day of my fast and basically just drinking water. I woke up feeling a bit faint, but the puffiness in my eyes and face was gone. I went to work and finally finished moving all the bales from the end of the barn to the chutes. Doing this while fasting was no easy task. All that remained now was to clean up the loose hay along the walls. I thought I could take care of that before leaving the monastery the following day.

During my noon break I ran into a monk loading firewood on to a wagon. I stopped to help him. It was Brother Donald, the other hermit—the one who prayed while Anthony wrote. Like Anthony, Donald was so full of energy and life it was infectious. I couldn't help but think that their seclusion had something to do with it. Or perhaps they really met so few people that when they came across somebody they just lit up. When we finished loading the wood Donald climbed up on the tractor to return to his hermitage, and I hitched a ride with him. I jumped off at the cross–roads, said good–bye, and continued on my walk. The smell of cedar and spruce was all around me and I slipped into serenity.

Back at the guest quarters, Anthony had sent word that he wanted to see me. I met him in the tea room later that afternoon. He counselled me to give things a chance to settle down in my life before making any major decisions about my job, about moving: be the best at what you do; accept the gift of Iain's return and Michelle's love; work at reconciling with Graeme and re–establishing Ruth's trust, he counselled.

"The knowledge you have is a gift. It has nothing to do with you," said Anthony. "After knowledge of this kind should come humility. If not, then the knowledge is in some sense faulty. Love was only in your mind. It was not profoundly felt. It was not in your heart. Christ sacrificed for you out of love. Iain saw that he couldn't do any more for you down here, so he went up there. He's sitting beside God right now."

Anthony's eyes gazed upward as this image unfolds.

"Well, God, we've got him this far," he said. "What do we do for him next?"

The image he had just conjured up was so beautiful that I could see Iain up there in my mind's eye. It was too much for me. I wept. Then I began to chuckle, the way Iain used to do, way deep down inside myself.

Anthony remained silent for a time and then recited a passage from Job 42 of Hebrew Scriptures:

Therefore I have uttered what I did
    not understand,
    things too wonderful for me,
    which I did not know.
'Hear, and I will speak;
    I will question you, and you declare it to me.'
I have heard of thee by the hearing of the ear,
    but now my eye sees thee;

Anthony has seen. The room in which he lives sometimes takes on a luminescent quality to him. He has come to see shades of differentiation and detail heretofore invisible to him. He hears the silence. He loves what he hears and sees. What he loves is the eternal in them. To him these presences are "God's works."

To me they are just presences, *Amawurrena* in a variety of Forms, and that is enough for me.

Day 8: None

This was my last day at the monastery. It was also the third day of my fast. Again, I woke up light–headed but relaxed. I attended Mass and then went to the barn to tidy up my work and say good–bye to Maurice and Leo. I was back in my room packing when a feeling swept over me that I had been here before. I mean, in this room, before I ever got here. I actually said it out loud, almost reflexively. As suddenly as the memory came, it went. I picked up my bag and went down to the reception desk to say good–bye to Roger.

It was mid–afternoon, and I was standing on the platform of the Rogersville train station wondering, "Where do I go from here?" I recalled my vow to Iain: "I'll stay, I won't go." It could mean many things.

*   *   *   *

My time at Notre Dame du Calvaire was the beginning of a journey because it was the end of one. My visit brought the worst of my grief and anxiety to an end. That grief and anxiety had driven away almost everyone who had tried to get close to me. Seeing they couldn't help, my closest friends took a step back, waiting for me to get through it. Not my daughter Michelle, though. She waded right in and took me by the hand and guided me along. She somehow knew what Anthony knew:

"Show calmness and compassion and the rest will take care of itself."

Now it was my turn.

I stayed overnight in Moncton with Francis. John had already returned to Toronto. The Bourques threw me a going–away party at their home that evening and invited a few of their relatives and friends over. Acadians all. They brought their guitars and singing voices and we sang well into the night.

*   *   *   *

After returning to Toronto from New Brunswick I prepared to leave for Australia to resume my work with the Aborigines. I had planned on travelling via New Zealand to visit Ellen, but after what had just happened in the monastery I decided not to, not yet anyway. It would be too much to handle. Instead I decided to travel via Singapore and attend a conference there before moving on to the Aborigines.

One evening, relaxing in my hotel room in Singapore with nothing in particular to do, I picked up the copy of *Teachings of the Buddha* in my desk drawer. This volume is to this part of the world what the Gideon Bible is to my part of the word. I sat down and started reading. And I did not set it down until I had finished. Something in it came as a revelation to me. I don't know why, because I was familiar with the basic teachings of Buddhism, but somehow the Buddhist notion of "detachment" suddenly made different sense to me. Along with many other commentators, particularly those of a Christian background, I had taken "detachment" to mean "removed from," "indifferent toward"—a kind of withdrawal from the world and other people. This made sense because "detachment" is one stage on the path to Enlightenment in the Buddhist tradition. One detaches oneself in an effort to free oneself from, well, worldly attachments. Sort of like the Trappist monks separated away in their monastery. Detachment is often used in this sense, but there is another sense in which it is used too. At a deeper level it means to detach *your own interest* in something or someone, that is, to perceive something or someone independently of your own personal interest in it. That is, to remove your ego from any consideration of it.

> 3. III. 1. Attachment to an ego–personality leads people into delusions, but faith in their Buddha–nature leads them to Enlightenment.

Detachment is to see the "other" in its own terms and to have compassion for it.

> 2.I.1 The Spirit of Buddha is that of great compassion and loving kindness. The great compassion is the spirit to save all people by any and all means. The great loving kindness is the spirit that prompts it to be ill with the illness of people, to suffer with their suffering.

Seen this way, detachment is a concept complementing the Christian notion of love—*how* to love. It is also a precondition for Aboriginal renunciation.

I realised that, until my experience of him in the barn at Notre Dame du Calvaire, I had not detached myself from Iain in the sense of detaching myself from *my* needs. It was still *my* grief, *my* loss I was dwelling on.

So then and there I started consciously to practice detachment, not only to ensure I really had let Iain go, but in relation to most other things around me. "See them for what they are independently of your interest in them," I kept telling myself. It sounds easy, but it is a really difficult thing to do on a day–to–day basis. If you stop and think just how much of your day consists of fulfilling your own needs, you'll know what I mean. But I set about trying.

When the time came to leave Singapore for Darwin I just could not get on the 'plane. I don't know if it had to do with these thoughts about "detachment" or about not wanting to re–live Iain's life with the Aborigines by going back there. But I didn't go. Instead, on an impulse, I decided to travel to nearby Bali in Indonesia. I needed a respite, a good dose of another culture to experience, even study, to take my mind and emotions off my problems.

I spent my last day in Singapore walking around the Chinese district. As I approached one of the many temples in the district I noticed a fortune–teller sitting on a blanket beside the gate. He was throwing small bones and seemed to be divining them for a customer. Beside him were cards and dice. His attention was on the pattern formed by each throw and I guessed him to be utilising the *I-ching*, or the *Book of Changes*, a work dating to the Confucian period whose origins go back some 3,000 years to the sages of the Taoist religion.

The *I-ching* contains sixty-four hexagrams representing all possible combinations of broken and unbroken lines. Each combination represents a particular quality or attribute of something. Water, for instance, is represented by two broken lines over one unbroken line over two broken lines, all on the horizontal. Sky is three parallel unbroken lines. Water over sky is hexagram number 5 and means "waiting" or patience. Each pattern, then, can be read to interpret a person's state of being or to recommend a certain state of being or course of action to them.

As I passed by the diviner he stopped what he was doing and spoke to me, beckoning me to sit down beside him. His customer seemed somewhat perplexed by this and promptly got up and left. The diviner now turned to me and said in halting English: "You know, don't you?" He picked up the bones and tossed them on the blanket. Then he said, "Sky and Earth. You have had bad luck, but things will get better in five to seven years. Then they will become exceptional. You should take care of your body. You will live to be at least 77. That's all." I reached into my pocket to pay him, but he beckoned it away. He just said, "Remember." I did. Earth over Sky is hexagon 12, "Obstruction," and consists of three parallel solid lines over three parallel broken ones. Blockage then release.

5

BALI

On the 'plane to Bali I was reading some materials I had picked up in Singapore about the country, its history and culture when the stewardess stopped beside me and pointed to a picture on the page I had turned to. "That's my temple," she said, "I belong to Tanah Lot." By now I knew that the Balinese not only belonged to a certain temple linked to their ancestral spirits but also belonged to a caste derived from the Indian Hindu system. I asked her what strata she belonged to. "Sudra," she replied.

Balinese caste divisions are the same as those of the Indian but there is no Harijan or Untouchable caste. The Balinese divisions are Brahmanas (Ida Bagus for men, Ida Ayu for women) the priest caste; Kshatriyas (Anak Agung Cokorde, Gusti or Sayu for men and Ni Gusti for women) the warrior and land–owning caste; Vaishya (Gusti for men, Si Luh for women), the merchant caste; and Sudra or the labouring caste. The first three castes are the "twice born" castes on the spiralling road of reincarnation on the way to *nirvana* or liberation from the earthly conditions of illusion (*maya*) and suffering. In Bali the twice born make up only about seven per cent of the population. They trace their origin to the rulers of the Hindu Majapahit kingdom who fled from Java to Bali in the fourteenth century to escape the expansion of Islam. The fourth caste, the Sudra, who have not yet entered the realm of the twice born in Bali, form the vast majority of the population. They are descendants of the original Bali Aga population and are mainly farmers and working people. In Bali, as in India, the Sudra may enter the realm of the twice–born and reach successive stages of reincarnation through worship, renunciation of worldly pursuits, and service. Good works are absorbed by one's *karma pala* which propels one's soul ever higher in each successive rebirth.

According to my readings, caste in Bali lacks the racial overtones of the Indian system which insists on marriage within the caste and ascribes caste membership on the basis of kinship or blood ties. Though the rule of marriage within the caste was adhered to until recently, the Balinese were able to alter their caste membership during their lifetime to, in effect, undermine this rule. This is because in Bali all people who worship at the same temple are regarded as members of the same caste and this includes women who have married in to the temple–worshipping group in question. People without a caste affiliation or who wish to change caste or sub–caste may set out to visit a number of temples until they sense the presence there of receptive ancestors which they then report to the temple community. A meeting determines whether the claim is justified and, if it is, the outsider is allowed in.

Nor in Bali are the twice born castes as politically and economically important as they are in India. Governance remains closely tied to the village and regional councils representing the community as a whole. Land is communally or individually owned without regard to caste, and with the importance of rice production and arts and crafts in the Balinese economy, the Sudra are as, if not more, prosperous than members of the other twice born castes. Caste distinctions, though, play an important social and ceremonial function in Bali which cannot be underestimated given the place of religion and ritual in Balinese life.

It seemed odd to me that there should be this little drop of Hinduism in the vast pool of Islam that engulfs the state of Indonesia. However, I had not realised how ancient was the tradition of Hinduism in this part of the world. My readings opened my eyes. There are records of Kshatriya and Brahmana castes in Bali prior to the sixth century and likely dating back to the second century. About 200 A.D. all of south–east Asia came under the influence of Hindu culture as a result of trade from India through the Straits of Malacca to Sumatra and Java. Brahmana priests and artists followed and converted the ruling chieftains to their religion. Between the third and thirteenth centuries, hundreds of Hindu kingdoms appeared in Indonesia, and by the tenth century a number of principalities had been established in Bali. The Indic system was superimposed on the indigenous Bali Aga people and their religion largely through the efforts of the principalities and their agents. The first written inscriptions from Bali in 881 A.D. mention distributing taxes for the establishment of hospices for the benefit of travellers, including monks from the royal court.

Hinduisation was followed in turn by a wave of Buddhist influence throughout Indonesia. This influence peaked in the sixth century but was not sufficiently strong to replace Hinduism which in turn had not been sufficiently strong to completely replace indigenous traditions. By the end of the tenth century political power was centred on the Hindu kingdom of Majapahit, only to wane in the wake of Islamic expansion in the region in the fourteenth century. By the end of the fifteenth century, politics in the region centred on the Islamic capital of Malacca which had gained control of maritime trade routes. But then in 1511 the Portuguese captured Malacca only to be replaced by the Dutch in 1596. The Dutch set up headquarters in Jakarta (Batavia) and reached Bali the following year.

From 1906 to 1908 the Dutch literally overran Bali and in doing so virtually wiped out the Balinese Kshatriya aristocracies of Badung and Klungkung principalities who, rather than surrender, chose to march unarmed straight into the gunfire of the enemy and then stabbed themselves to death if they survived. This was referred to as "Puntun" or "The Finish" and reflected the Balinese belief that European invasion heralded the end of the world. However, the Dutch, in turn, were expelled from Bali and Indonesia during World War II when Indonesia became an independent state. My introductory history lesson complete, we landed in Denpasar.

Kuta

Both feet on the ground, I realised I didn't really have any plan and I didn't know anybody here. Even so, I resolved to persist with this detour in my travels and just go with the flow. The taxi driver found me a hotel in Kuta, a beach area south of the city which, he said, was popular with the Australians. Australians flock here in their winter, many to surf and many more just to party. They tend to be young and rowdy so I wasn't so sure this hotel was a good idea, given my agitated state of being. However, two Australian women I met at breakfast the next morning told me not to worry, the partying went on in the nearby bars, not in the hotel. If I really wanted peace and quiet, they said, Denpasar was not the place to be. I should get out into the countryside. It wasn't just the foreign tourists, it was the Javanese hawkers who had come here to exploit the tourist trade. They hung out around the hotels and on the beach selling trinkets, souvenirs and sex.

When I went down to the beach later that day I found out what they were talking about. First one, then another, hawker peddling cheap *batik*, the local hand–woven cotton cloth, crude paintings, and "massages" from women back of the beach in the dunes. This was no place for me so I quickly walked inland away from the beach. Soon I was in the countryside away from all the commotion. Inland the vegetation thickened and varieties of palms formed a canopy that gave shelter from the heat and exuded an earthy, organic, fragrance that filled my senses with life. Suddenly the jungle broke into a clearing and opened onto a field where a group of women were winnowing tapioca. Without really thinking of the etiquette of it, I beckoned to them that I would like to help. They seemed somewhat startled by my sudden appearance and puzzled as to my request, but then one of the women smiled and handed me a stick, and so I pitched in. After about an hour or so, one of the women went to a nearby house and returned with some drinks and a pineapple which she offered around. Afterwards, the one who had given me the stick said in English, "It's time for you to go back to Kuta now, it is a long walk." I took my leave having thoroughly enjoyed this wordless form of communion.

On the way back I stopped at a drink shop and got into a conversation with a young man from Sumatra who also spoke good English. I don't know what it is about grief or pain, but it somehow seeks itself out in others around you—and theirs in you. Nothing need be said—indeed you may actively be trying to keep your pain from showing—but somehow it communicates and connects. His mother, whom he had loved very much, had died and his father had taken a second wife with two children who set about alienating his father from him. It reached the point where he had to leave home and had come to Bali looking for work. However, he missed his father very much and wished he could go back. I replied with my own story and we parted, somehow each comforted by the plight of the other.

I don't know how I managed to get lost after that, but I did. All roads did not, as I mistakenly thought, lead back to Kuta and my hotel. The path I was on was leading me into thick bush rather than open ground when suddenly I realised I was in the precinct of a temple, or at least the ruins of a temple. The stone foundation was partly overgrown, and there were no pagoda towers such as are typical of Balinese temples. I was about to take my leave of the place when I noted offerings of flowers and food on a stone platform atop the steps in front of me. I climbed up and took out my camera to take a picture but as I did a young man stepped out of the shadows and beckoned me to stop. I did and he politely took me back down the steps and outside the compound. To my surprise I found myself looking at the ocean. I had walked in a circle. I turned to thank the young man for his trouble and perhaps question him about the ruins, but he was gone.

The next morning at the hotel I met Sally and Libby, the two Auzzie women again, this time accompanied by their "chaperones" Mike and Daphne. Libby was Sally's sister–in–law and they were here without their husbands but with their aunt and her friend on holidays. They invited me to come with them to Lake Bratan later in the week. Lake Bratan is due north of Kuta in the mountainous north–centre of the island. It is one of four crater lakes of special significance to the Balinese. The others are Lake Batur, Lake Bujan. and Lake Tamblingan. Lake Bratan is just south of Mt. Catur, one of Bali's sacred mountains, which rises to 7,011 ft. (2,137m.). The principal sacred mountain of Bali is Mt. Agung to the east which is 10,308 ft. (3,142 m.). Others are Mt. Batukau (7,707 ft. or 2,349 m.), Mt. Abang (7,054 ft. or 2,150 m.) and Mount Batur (5,633 ft. or 1,717 m). Mt. Agung erupted in 1963 and Mt. Batur in 1917. North of the mountains is dry, arid, country mostly unsuitable to agriculture. The fertile lands and most of the population are found to the south where rice is grown and fruits such as papaya, bananas, jackfruit, and many varieties of palms are found in abundance. Bali is only 172 miles (277 km.) long by 102 miles (164 km.) wide to begin with and if you subtract the arid north and mountainous centre and you can see that most of Bali's two and a half million people are compressed into a very small living space indeed.

It was not so hot nor so crowded in the mountains and I was looking forward to cooling off and having some space. Our driver was a young Balinese man, Ketut Senaca, who also acted as our guide. Lake Bratan is about 2 miles (3 km.) across, and along its length it is bordered by forests with mountains rising to the east and west. On the western edge of the lake on a promontory jutting out into the lake itself is Pura Candikuning—a beautiful temple in the classical Balinese style. Our approach by boat from the far end of the lake was mesmerising. Two *merus* or pagodas with their thatched platforms successively pyramiding toward the sky slowly emerged into view. These *merus*, Ketut told us, represented the sacred mountains each of which formed a stairway from earth to heaven. Drawing closer we could see that the promontory was in fact a small island at the end of a small peninsula, the latter supporting an 11–platformed pagoda, the former a three–platformed one dedicated to the rice goddess Dewi Sri. We disembarked and were surprised to find the temple empty aside from a few visitors like ourselves. No priests, no ceremonial objects, no statues, nothing. Ketut explained:

In contrast to Hindu temples in India, in Bali the deities are absent except on festival occasions when they are recalled for the purpose. In Bali it is the spirits of the deities who are worshipped, not the deities themselves. Spirits are never seen. The temples, then, are venues for mediating the unseen world of the spirits and the seen world experienced by humans. In them are enacted ancient forms of music, dance, and drama which recount events from the time when the gods walked among men and shaped the way life is and should be today. These events are recounted in Hindu mythology in the great epics, the Mahabharata and Ramayana.

When we returned to Kuta I asked the others if they would like to take another trip in a few days to visit other temples and places. However, they had made other plans, so I asked Ketut if he would take me on tour himself, making a circuit through the central part of the island to the north coast and back again by a more westerly route. We left on Monday and made our way north to Pejeng, Tampaksiring, Besakih near Mt. Agung, past Mt. Batur to Sansit on the north coast then back via Ketut's home village of Chaumarga (photo 14) on the western edge of the central mountain range.

Pejeng hosts one of Bali's national Temples, Pura Panataram Sasih one of whose shrines houses the "Moon Face Drum" dating from the ninth century. Legend has it that the drum fell to this spot from the sky when a thief, wishing a cover of darkness under which to ply his trade, ascended to the heavens and knocked down one of the two moons there. At Tampaksiring we witnessed an offering ceremony to the Hindu gods, Brahman, Vishnu, and Shiva. Brahman is the creator, Vishnu the preserver of life, Shiva the dissolver of matter to release spirit. The procession was a colourful one indeed. The women wore elaborately patterned ankle–length skirts made from *kain* or *batik* wrapped tightly around the waist and held by a sash. The men wore a *sarong* costume extending from the waist to just below the knees tied in front to form a double overlap. With them was a small *gamelan* percussion orchestra. The air was filled with music and the fragrance of flowers and I fell into a mild kind of trance as we watched the company pass by. What broke the spell was the sight of a reverse swastika symbol born on a banner by one of the participants. For me that brought to mind the Nazis, World War II, the holocaust. For Ketut and the participants, however, it meant something quite different. In the Hindu tradition the reverse swastika represents well–being, its four arms different stages in the cycle of rebirth. The upper arm, said Ketut, symbolises Brahman and the purifying power of fire; the middle arm Vishnu and water, the source of life; and the lower arm Shiva.

By noon we had ascended to the edge of the caldera which contains Lake Batur from where we hoped to view Mt. Agung to the south–east, but clouds obscured even its volcanic cone. We were rewarded instead with the vista below us—a vast basin or crater some 6.8 miles (11 km.) across on the eastern part of which is Lake Batur. Vegetation around the lake is sparse due to lava flow and no settlements are to be seen along the western side of the lake, a legacy of the eruption of 1926 which destroyed the village of Batur.

From Batur we made our way past Mt. Panulusan and began our descent to the northern coast and the town of Tamblang. The forest here is dense with ferns and casuarina stands which slowly give way to coffee plantations and taro gardens and then to rice terraces and coconut palms. As we approached Tamblang I noticed roosters in baskets sitting beside the road. I asked Ketut what they were doing there and he said they were being prepared for cockfighting by being exposed to traffic and noise. This way they would not be distracted by the noise of the crowd when it came time to fight. For the most part the countryside beyond Tamblang is dry and dusty except in the vicinity of Singaraja and Seririt. Life here seemed unspectacular compared to the south and temples more often than not seemed unkempt, overrun with vines and vegetation, and unused.

Perhaps unfairly, we did not linger long in the north but made our way south by way of Git Git Falls and Lake Bratan. But on the way we made a detour to pay a brief visit to Ketut's parents in the village of Chaumarga (photo 14). Chaumarga lies to the west of the main road from Lake Bratan as it descends to the southern lowlands. The region is fertile and suitable for rice–cultivation as well as a variety of vegetables and fruits. Ketut's father, though, is the local school teacher. A quick tour around the village before we met his parents revealed a ground plan which is typical of Bali: domestic compounds, a village temple (*pura desa*), an assembly hall (*bale agung*), an arena (*wantilan*), a market, a village bell or *kulkul* and a sacred banyan tree (*waringin*). It was late afternoon and the place was bustling as men and women returned from the fields and other destinations. The air was sweet with the fragrance of flowers and the aroma of spices. It's funny what you notice—the cats in the doorways. None of them had any tails! I mentioned this to Ketut. Cats and geese, he said, are sacred to the Balinese. They don't want the cats to be accidentally killed so they take the animals out into the middle of the road amidst the traffic and cut off their tails. From then on the cats associate the road with pain and avoid it.

We made a brief stop at Ketut's parents' home to pick up some things to take into town. I was introduced as a "Professor" from Canada, Ketut's new friend. If I had time, his parents said, I should come back for a longer stay. On the way back to Kuta, though, Ketut said that this might be difficult as the authorities did not like foreigners staying in remote villages. It wasn't the Balinese but the central government in Jakarta who controlled the local police, many of whom were Javanese imports.

These two trips to the countryside revealed to me that side of Bali that has held visitors captive for over half a century—mountains, temples, rice fields, artisans, music and an endless parade of festivals. The contrast with Kuta could not be more striking. For instance, a couple of nights later I was invited out by Sally and Libby to the *Bounty*. Would you believe a mock–up version of Bligh's *Bounty* in the middle of Kuta showing two movies a night while serving drinks to three decks of passengers? Almost all of them were Australians in their early twenties. I left early and walked back to the hotel. As I did a young Javanese man approached me in the street and asked if I wanted a Balinese woman—he was very specific.

I had to get out of here.

Candi Dasa

The next day I went to the tourist office in Denpasar and asked if there were places to stay in the eastern part of the island in the district of Klungkung, one of the more traditional areas. I found a place on the beach in Candi Dasa and planned to set out at the end of the week. That afternoon I went to the market in Denpasar and learned something about doing business in Bali. Bargaining is expected, but there are certain rules you are expected to follow. You start by offering a sum two–thirds below the asking price, then the dealer comes down as you go up, arriving together somewhere in the middle. But the dealer always has a bottom line price which they think is fair and if you stop bargaining below that price and stay there, they get very annoyed indeed. A piece of *batik* I wanted, for instance, was r7500 (about $3 Can). I countered r2000 and she responded, "5000." I said, "3000," she said "5000." I said "4000" and she just folded it up and put it away. I came back later and paid r5000.

It was there that I came across this almost life–sized carving of a Balinese tiger, lying there curled up just like the real thing. Actually there are few if any of the real thing left in Bali due to the pressures of human settlement. The Balinese tiger is called *machangtutul* (*tutul* for short) and is spotted rather than striped. The carved tiger seemed to smile at me, and I saw something in the visage that startled me. I swear I caught a glimpse of a person's face there when viewed from a certain angle. The impression was fleeting but unmistakable. (Later, back home when I meditated on the tiger, I discovered three faces—the tiger's, a small human face of a young man on the right side of the face and a larger human face of an older man on the left. I imagine the younger one to be the artist and the older his teacher but, of course, I have no way of knowing.) In the spirit of the occasion I bargained, but not enthusiastically and ended up buying the tiger at about the vendor's "bottom line." Even so, I went away as happy as she did.

The next day I was off to Candi Dasa after saying good–bye to

Sally and Co. I really appreciated their company and was sorry to leave them, but I really wanted to see more of traditional Bali.

As you reach Giyanyar the vegetation grows lush and dense, the air organic. The warmth and life of it enfolds you and penetrates your every pore.

The hotel was modest and right on the beach, but filled with tourists like me though this time not quite so many Australians. Mostly Europeans and English. The Auzzies in Kuta might have been loud and boisterous, but at least they were convivial and easy to get along with. The Europeans here, though, were more stand–offish and aloof, preferring to keep to themselves. They seemed to spend most of their time sunbathing. The fact that they sunbathed naked did not endear them to the local Balinese who found that offensive. I did meet an English threesome on "permanent vacation" to Egypt, India, Thailand, Indonesia, and Australia. Jackie, one of the trio, had been very impressed with Dharamsala in India. This is the home–in–exile of the Dalai Lama, the spiritual leader of Tibet, and of a community of Tibetan refugees. Everybody, she said, was always smiling. It made you happy and you felt guilty because you hadn't done anything to deserve it. Now *that's* English!

Saturday night I attended a local performance of the Barong dance. The Barong depicts the eternal battle between good and evil, symbolised by Barong, a mythical Chinese lion, and evil symbolised by Queen Durga. The play opens with a prologue to introduce the Barong and his band of monkey friends. The lion is a magnificent beast indeed and is manipulated by two men, one in the head and the other the tail. The prologue is followed by a *legong* or classical dance by two women. Then comes the play itself. Prince Sadewa is to be sacrificed to Betari Durga, the Goddess of Death. However, Lord Shiva appears and gives Sadewa immortality. Durga tries to kill him but now, of course, cannot. Finally she asks Sadewa to destroy her so she can return to Shiva as his wife. Then a disciple of Durga's appears and also asks to be sacrificed by Sadewa, but he refuses. They fight. After a series of struggles Sadewa enlists the aid of the Barong, but they cannot subdue her. The Barong in turn calls on the *kris* (ceremonial dagger) dancers to help him but they too are unsuccessful. In frustration they turn their weapons on themselves but are disarmed before they can cause harm.

Like most Balinese theatre and art, the Barong is rooted in Indian Hindu religion and mythology, specifically the Mahabharata and Ramayana epics. In these epics the struggles of the gods and human dynasties are indistinguishable, with the gods alternatively intervening and withdrawing from human affairs—much as in Greek mythology—but always leaving moral messages for humankind. In a performance of scenes from the Ramayana I witnessed a few days later, Rama, the legal heir to the throne of Dasaratha, has been exiled from Ayodhia by his father, on the wishes of one of his wives. Together with his wife Sinta and his brother Laksamana, Rama withdraws to the forest. His brother, Bharata who is now first in line for the throne, returns home to find his father dead from grief and begs Rama to return. Rama, though, remains true to his father's command and stays in exile asking Bharata to rule in his place. But Sinta is kidnapped by another king, Rahwana, who appears in the form of a golden deer. With the aid of Hanoman, the sacred white monkey, Rama defeats Rahwana, recovers his wife and returns to Ayodhia. The moral? Not fealty or loyalty to your king as it might be in European mediaeval lore, but rather "act according to *dharma* or what is right," in a larger, cosmological sense.

This is the also theme of the Baghavad Gita, an eighteen–chapter segment of the Mahabharata epic, where Lord Krishna, the incarnation of Vishnu, instructs Arjuna of the Pandavas on his duty to fight on the eve of battle, even though he faces his kinsmen and friends on the other side (the Kauravas). The Pandavas had lost everything in a game of dice between their king Yudhisthira and Duryodhana of the Kauravas and had spent 13 years in exile on the promise their lands and titles would be restored thereafter. They returned but Duryodhana refused to honour his promise. Krishna's efforts at compromise have failed and war now seems inevitable. Krishna tells Arjuna he must do his duty and act selflessly in accord with *dharma* or divine order embodied in Krishna.

Though the nature of this "divine order" is not explicitly stated, it is immediately apparent when one realizes how "renunciation" works: the Pandavas have lost everything (indeed by refusing to quit the game as it proceeds seem intentionally bent on losing everything) and now have nothing. The Kauravas now have everything (both their own and the Panadavas'). By renunciative logic the Panadvas are now entitled to everything (both what was theirs and the Kauravas') and, indeed, "right action" will settle for nothing less. (Krishna himself, by the way, himself embodies renunciation in the sense that he is Divine (spirit) and constantly gives every thing away that comes into his possession). In order to fulfil the divine order, then, Arjuna must fight to gain "everything" for the Panadavas while eliminating the deviant Kauravas from the process. This is precisely what happens.

The Mahabharata and Ramayana are, of course, Indian tales and Indian ethics imported into Bali. Balinese religion is Hindu, but it rests on indigenous, Bali Aga, foundations. In the Bali Aga religion, Bali is viewed as the whole world floating on the ocean supported by a great turtle and entwined snakes (much as in Native North American lore). Sun, earth, and water are worshipped as the source of life and fire as the purifying element. Mountains are regarded as holy and the source of well–being and fertility. The holiest of the mountains is Mt. Agung, the navel of the world and the place from which the ancestral spirits periodically return to earth as honoured guests (and the place where the god Vishnu now resides). Every temple and household shrine in Bali provides for the propitiation of the mountains and their deities.

Balinese religion conceives of God but not really in the Muslim or Christian sense, though the Balinese will often pay lip service to the monotheistic Muslim notion of Allah to placate the Indonesian authorities. The Balinese conceive *Sanghyang Widhi Wasa* as an omnipotent life force beyond the mundane world of good and evil, life and death. In the tradition of Hinduism, though, they see this life force as personified by the Trinity of Brahman, Vishnu, and Shiva.

Balinese religion draws a distinction between the visible and invisible realms of existence and then declares them to be interpenetrating. As Frederik Barth puts it (in *Balinese Worlds*, Chicago: University of Chicago Press, 1994). "it is a world of immaterial entities and forces as much as one of material objects; a world of invisible agents that surround us and even enter us; a world alive with gods and spirits and ogres and holy priests. It is hardly possible to exaggerate the extent to which the unseen penetrates the seen" (page 192).

The universe is divided into two orders, the macrocosmos (Bwana

Agung) and the microcosmos (Bwana Alit) and three worlds, the Upper of the gods (of growth), the Lower of demons (of decay), and the Middle of humans whose purpose is to maintain the other two worlds in balance so that decay does not overwhelm growth, nor evil overtake good. The problems for humans is that they do not have access to the unseen world and thus do not know how to achieve this balance, let alone move into it in the cycle of rebirth.

Humans live in a Middle World of *maya* or illusion that masks the true nature of reality. It is *maya* that causes them to make mistakes in relation to the unseen world and that prevents their escape from suffering, separating as it does *samsara* (appearance) from *nirvana* (the absolute). *Maya* moves like the shadowy figures in a Balinese *wayang* puppet play, concealing more than it reveals and revealing more than it conceals. In one of the most ancient of Hindu texts, the Rig Veda, *maya* refers to the deceptive power of the gods. In the Upanishads, a later text, it is a force wielded by Brahman to mask nature with appearances.

One breaks through *maya* by proper instruction in the Hindu faith and by "seeing." To "see" is not to be taught to believe something but to experience it directly by suspending the use of intellect. "Seeing" is an act of sensing, not just with the eyes but with the ears, the nose and the heart. Thinking, or the intellect, is more than just a barrier to understanding the ultimate, it is *maya* itself. The intellect freezes and distorts reality by turning it into categories. It then proceeds to analyse as if the categories were reality itself. Another aspect of "seeing" is renunciation in the Buddhist sense—surrendering all attachments and desires in compassionate service to one's fellows. In other words, opening up oneself to "other" by obliterating the ego aspect of one's self. Seeing to the Hindu ascetic is what silence and prayer is to the Trappist monks and what music and meditation are to the Aborigines.

The invisible world beyond *maya* is something that "resonates" around and within us and can be sensed and intuited under certain circumstances. To the Balinese, an immediate sense of this world can be gained by intuiting one's spiritual self and bringing it into "aesthetic tune" with the visible part of oneself—that is, one's appearance. This is accomplished by the way one dresses, moves, and generally comports oneself. To the degree that one achieves this representation accurately, one is protected from the influence of evil spirits and sorcery, that is, from possession by an evil agent of the spirit world. With one's spiritual essence properly represented, one naturally assumes a joyful heart and avoids sadness that leads to weakness and vulnerability. Hence the renowned "beauty" of the Balinese people, a beauty that is, in a sense, less than skin deep.

Circumstances in which the invisible world can be accessed are circumstances of transition where the line between the two worlds becomes blurred such as on death. Mortuary ceremonies in Bali, as in Australia, function to reunite the visible and invisible by purifying the soul of the deceased before releasing it to the Upper World and ultimate reality (*moksha* or *nirvana*). This is effected by cremation utilising the sacred element of fire. Cremation ceremonies in Bali are spectacular and joyful affairs as this is a time for celebrating the progress of the spirit and for accessing, for a moment, the invisible world, not for lamenting the loss of a loved one. The body or its effigy is carried atop a huge tower (*wadah*) of wood and bamboo constructed in three tiers to represent the levels of the universe. At the cemetery everything is ritually purified by burning; the ashes are collected and then scattered on the sea along with offerings.

Certain individuals occupy a permanently liminal position in relation to the invisible world either as an accident of birth or of training. These are the shamans (*balan*). These are special individuals who have been given the power of *sakti*, the ability to draw on the powers of the invisible world for the purpose of healing, a power attainable only by men. One of these powers of healing is the ability to exorcise evil spirits called *bhutas* and *kalas* from people's bodies. I witnessed a public exorcism at a distance while driving one day with Ketut, but he would not stop for fear we would be contaminated, not by the spirits involved, but by the frenzy of the crowd who acted out the exorcism along with the patient and healer.

The more I experienced of Balinese religion and the more I delved into it in my readings and in conversations with visitors and local Balinese, the more intrigued I became. In a way it was therapeutic, discovering a theology—a philosophy, a cosmology—that fit with what the Aborigines were trying to teach me and with my own experience of the "seen" and the "unseen" worlds, particularly in connection with Iain. For an instant I had broken through the veil of *maya* to "see" a reality beyond consciousness, and now I was learning how to "see" more clearly in general apart from the intellectual apparatuses I had built into myself for interpreting the world. I would not backslide, not if I could help it.

It was July 17th, the day before my birthday. I decided to rent a bicycle and visit Goa Lawah, the Bat Cave near Kusamba about 19 miles (30 km.) away. On the way I took a small detour down to Padang where the ferry to Lombok docks. On the beach some men were building a boat that looked very familiar to me. I stopped and went over, pointed to the craft and said, *yibalyiba*. This is the Aboriginal name for the smaller boats that the Macassans brought with them on their *praus* or sailboats when they visited the shores of northern Australia from Indonesia hundreds of years before European contact. The Aborigines said that the word derived from the Macassan language. However, the boat builder replied "*prau*" to my question. Nevertheless, *yibalyiba*, is what it was to me, and I felt as if I had suddenly made connection with my Aboriginal friends on Groote Eylandt.

Bicycling is the way to go in Bali, at least on the lowlands. That organic feeling again with the scent of soil, coconut milk, and spices when you pass through a settlement. When on bicycle the Balinese smile and speak to you, sometimes in English, sometimes in Balinese. It was here that I noticed the Balinese smile. It wasn't the Balinese smile I was used to in the hotels and tourist traps but something different. The Balinese smile at tourists like the tourists smile at each other, usually with a broad grin with the mouth slightly open. I guess it's good for business or they are natural–born mimics. However, amongst themselves they raise the face and the eyebrows slightly and offer a small grin. When I did this myself to the Balinese I met on my trip, I found that they responded in kind, and treated me less as a tourist. It kind of broke down a barrier.

Bicycling put me in the mood to reflect. I wished my children were with me, but the thought did not trigger grief as it had so many times before. The edge seemed to have come off. Instead I thought about what I could bring back for them and my fiends. A *kris*? a *sarong*? a painting?

The Bat Cave houses bats—millions of them. At the entrance is a shrine where one propitiates the gods of the cave which I did, but the stench of bat dung dissuaded me from proceeding much further. Anyway, when you've seen or heard one bat you've seen or heard them all.

The next day was my birthday and I was taken out to dinner by Peter, an Australian I met in Candi Dasa who was deputy vice-chancellor of the University of Tasmania. The strange thing was, he knew who I was. "You're the bloke on the Sunday Morning programme, aren't you? The Canadian involved with the Strehlow collection?" Channel 9 television in Sydney had done a 60 Minutes-type documentary on "Australia's Crown Jewels," the largest and best-documented collection of Aboriginal artefacts— written records, tapes, and photographs—ever assembled in Australia. Much of it had been given to Professor T.G.H. Strehlow by Aranda elders in central Australia in the 1950s and 1960s when they foresaw the loss of their culture and the degeneration of their young people at the hands of Europeans. The controversy began when Professor Strehlow turned the collection into a private research institute and, in order to raise money, published photographs of secret–sacred Aranda ceremonies in *Der Stern* magazine in Germany and *People* magazine in Australia. To make a long story short, Professor Strehlow died shortly thereafter and left the collection to his second wife, Kathy. Since most of the collection dealt with secret men's business from which women were excluded this only made matters worse. I entered in as someone whose work on Aborigines Professor Strehlow had respected and who understood something of his predicament, having basically been shut out of the Australian anthropological establishment myself long before the collection was ever an issue. *Der Stern* had reneged on an agreement to keep the photos out of Australia and had sold rights to them to *People*. Strehlow had wrongly assumed that all the Aborigines connected with the materials in the collection had died along with the Aranda's ceremonies. When the pictures appeared Strehlow was denounced, his reputation shattered. I was brought over to Adelaide by Strehlow's Foundation to assess the academic value of the collection and, after considerable intrigue and hesitation on the part of Kathy, helped formulate an agreement between her and the Northern Territory Government (represented by

Barry Coulter) to turn over the collection to them. It is now being held in trust for Aboriginal people in a facility in Alice Springs.

So Peter and I spent the evening hashing over the ins and outs, the rights and wrongs, of this episode of Australian history while I turned 48. Considering the viciousness of the politics of the Strehlow affair, perhaps it was appropriate that the next day I should witness my first cockfight—at Bugbug, the next town to the east. Cockfighting is illegal in Bali because gambling is illegal and cockfighting exists mainly for the purpose of gambling. However, cockfighting persists, and officialdom in most cases turns a blind eye. As the event begins the owners take their cocks from their cages and display them to the crowd, revealing in stages the quality of their birds in order to build up excitement and enthusiasm—and to manipulate the odds. Challenges are made between owners, the odds are set, the crowd surges forward to the fighting circle as the birds are fitted with razor sharp spurs bound to the feet, owners and birds taunt each other as the crowd leans forward and shouts encouragement to their favourite. Then the birds are released, there's a brief flurry of activity as they fly at each other and then it's over, one left standing, the other usually dead. In a sense the fight itself (for the spectators at least) is anti-climactic as the real interest is in all the commotion leading up to the fight. A good bird can last for as many as 10 fights before being killed, and make a lot of money for its owner. Unfortunately for the birds, there's no mandatory retirement policy.

Later that week I hired a taxi and drove to Besakih temple (photo 18) on the slopes of Mount Agung, just to the north of us. Besakih is the Mother Temple, Bali's oldest and its most sacred. It consists almost entirely of thatched, pagoda–style *merus* built up the slope toward Mount Agung. It is indeed a magnificent sight, particularly when seen from the approach where its pagodas appear highlighted against a backdrop of mountains. Tradition dates the oldest of these *merus* to the second century and attributes its construction to the Hindu seer Sri Maharkadia who brought that religion to Bali and gave Bali its name. Besakih plays host to the principal gods of Bali, to the spirits of the ancient seers and of the ancestors, and contains precincts for each of the old Balinese states or provinces and the various sects of Hinduism. Like all Balinese temples, Besakih is a point of mediation between the seen and the unseen worlds where, for a moment during a festival when the spirits are recalled, the veil of *maya* or illusion is penetrated.

Stephen Lansing (in *Three Worlds of Bali*, New York: Praeger, 1983, pages 7–8) remarks that

> Temples form links between the human world and the unseen worlds of Indic cosmology, which postulates that events in the human (Middle) world are continuously influenced by the upper worlds of gods and ancestral spirits and by the lower world of demonic powers . . . The success of human undertakings, literally from birth to death, depends upon keeping the forces of these two worlds in balance, which is the primary purpose of every temple festival.

> Temples are where communal offerings are made to the gods to maintain a balance of forces in the universe. The gifts must be substantial in the form of food, flowers, and money but only their spiritual essence is consumed by the gods. The material aspect is taken home and consumed by the villagers.

> In Bali there are over 20,000 of these temples. Each village contains several dozen, each of a certain kind serving a different purpose such as farming temples, water temples, caste temples, and state temples. However, there is always a base of the three in all villages: Pura Puseh, dedicated to the worship of Vishnu, the preserver of life, set to the north; Pura Dalem, for Shiva, the dissolver of matter to release spirit, set to the south; and Rura Desa, for Brahman the creator, set to the middle. As with caste divisions, most Balinese temples cross–cut village and regional borders to link people and bring them into interaction on festival occasions.

> One cannot underestimate the importance of the temples and temple festivals in the everyday life of the Balinese. For example, certain water temples called *pura masceti* house ancient calendars which determine the opening and closing of irrigation canals which in turn co–ordinate water use for entire regions and hence determine the economic productivity of the land and of the villagers. These *pura masceti* are located at the water source of a number of *subak* temples, each a place where people whose lands are watered by the same upstream dam congregate. Smaller temples (*tempek*) are located on canals within the *subak* area in turn. *Subak* members at each plateau of a watercourse congregate periodically at the *pura masceti* to check that they are all conforming to the ritual planting cycle which is staggered to accommodate each level on the watercourse. In this way the interests of all are ensured, and each receives his or her yield.

In the 1960s western economic models adopted by the Indonesian government sought to change this system in a more "scientific" direction. Lansing discusses the results:

> The delicate ecological balance achieved by the water temple system was underlined recently by several ill–fated attempts to abandon the system in several districts in south Bali. Following the advice of modernising experts, farmers abandoned the ritual scheduling of activities and planted as often as possible, using fertiliser and insecticides to increase productivity. A steady diet of rice became available to predators such as rodents and insects, whose numbers were kept down in the old system by the regular district–wide breaks in planting when fields were left to fallow. Soil conditions changed, fields became harder to plough, irrigation became haphazard, and productivity declined. By 1979, nearly all the farmers involved had returned to the system of scheduled planting by temple calendars. (page 60)

One does indeed mess with the sacred calendar at one's own peril. On gaining independence in 1949, President Sukarno declared his five preconditions for the achievement of Indonesian nationhood: one God, nationalism, humanitarianism, social justice and democracy. Balinese Hinduism has, of course, many Gods or deities deriving from Indian Hindu mythology, whereas Islam, of course, recognises one and only one. Furthermore, nationalism for Sukarno meant a unitary state based on the Javanese model. This could have meant assimilation for Bali but for the worldwide reputation it had now gained for its beauty and cultural uniqueness—and for the tourist dollars that could be siphoned off by the Indonesian state. So Bali's traditions were permitted to continue, but this did not prevent the state from meddling in Balinese affairs when it suited its purposes.

Eka Dasa Rudra is a once–a–century purification ceremony held to ensure the well–being of the entire Middle World. Such a ceremony was scheduled in 1963 but with much controversy as there were conflicting ideas about whether or not this was the appropriate year. As plans stalled President Sukarno intervened and insisted the ceremony proceed as he wished to use it as a platform on which to introduce his "New Order" political and economic development programme, administered, of course, from Jakarta. As preparations were getting under way, Mount Agung erupted. Still Sukarno insisted that the ceremony proceed. Then lava began to pour down the mountain. Sukarno cancelled his appearance, and the Balinese cancelled the ceremony. The eruption worsened, and many villages were destroyed. All of this was interpreted as a divine judgement on the Sukarno regime and indeed his government fell in a bloody coup in 1965.

*   *   *   *

Having by now some background reading and some life experience of Bali behind me, I decided to return to Kuta and check with Ketut about taking up his parents' offer to visit his home at Chaumarga. Perhaps alone as an unsuspecting tourist I would escape the gaze of the authorities.

Speaking of Ketut, I had observed on my trip that there were a great many "Ketuts" about. I asked my Ketut about it when I saw him. "Was it like Smith in English?" No. Names, he said, are given according to order of birth and they are the same names for all Balinese The first child is Wayan, the second Made, the third Nyoman and the fourth Ketut (or the parallel sequence Putu, Kadek, Komang and Ketut.) As my Ketut said, this can be very confusing for the foreigner when he or she is trying to identify and locate someone. Though the Balinese have other names they are not used in general conversation. Ketut's full name is *I* (boy; girl is *ni*) Ketut (3rd born) Guday (big) Ginastra (fire arrow of the god Arjuna) Wiyaya (winner). The names Ginastra and Wiyaya were inherited from his father which was, as Ketut explained it, an act of "giving a part of himself to me."

Giving a part of oneself to someone else is something the Balinese do every day in the very act of speaking to each other. Bali boasts not one but five languages, each used by the same person for different purposes. Basa Lumrah is used when speaking to people of the same caste as well as family and friends. Basa Sor is used to address non twice–born persons of a lower level. Basa Singgih is used to address superiors of higher standing. Basa Madia is the language of courtesy and is the most commonly used of the five by all castes. Basa Alus is used amongst the more literate and cultured of the Balinese and derives from Sanskrit. Once it is determined by using the common language that one speaker is high caste and the other low, the low caste person will address the high caste person in the high tongue and the high caste person will address the low caste one in the low tongue. Rather than expressing a relation of subordination or superiority it is rather a marker of interdependence. "My high caste language is for you speaking to me and your low caste language is for me speaking to you." That is, one actually "owns" a language in order to renounce it to someone else for their own use. To me, this is a very Aboriginal practice.

Chaumarga

We drove to Chaumarga Friday evening after Ketut finished work. It was about 8 p.m. when we came upon small groups of people sitting beside the road talking. Then ahead we saw a large group congregated about a caravan. Ketut said it was Jogat Bumbung, Dancing Boy and Girl. It was a dance held after the harvest festival to relax everyone. I soon found out why. The caravan belonged to a dance troupe of women who dressed and acted the part of courtesans to the men of the village who paid to dance with them, one at a time. The idea behind the dance was quite simply, seduction. The man danced advances at the woman and the woman alternatively danced encouragement and discouragement back. If the man danced too close to her, she would back away but in such a way as to encourage another advance. The dancing was traditional or classical Balinese style with gestures added to suit the context. The aim of the dance for the men was to perform well enough to receive a kiss on the cheek from the "courtesan" as a finale. The assembled crowd were as much a part of the dance as the dancers themselves, oohing and ahhing when the man managed to gain an advantage on the woman, and sighing and bemoaning when she escaped his advance and began the cycle again. Then, late in the evening, an old man appeared in the circle. The crowd uttered an ahhhh . . . and I realised this was to be something special. The old man danced differently from the others. Ketut said it was old Balinese style. His every movement spoke grace and subtlety. Even the "courtesan" seemed mesmerised. It seemed as if the roles had been reversed and it was she who was trying to seduce him. Then, toward the end, he moved his hand toward her and held it behind her bottom but without touching her. She allowed the movement and the crowd erupted with laughter and applause. The dance was over. She gave him a kiss on the cheek. However, there was to be one more before the evening ended—me. Ketut said that the villagers insisted and that it would be an affront not to accept the invitation. Well, I am no dancer, certainly not in this country, but I had watched the proceedings and noted some "moves" so why not?

I took something akin to a traditional pose with my knees bent, arms raised, hand pointing out in opposite directions—a kind of Dancing Shiva pose—and the crowd roared. What next? The music began and she danced toward me. Unsure, I began to dance toward her, but then I noticed her eyes. She was leading me, first a glance to the right then to the left, then at my hand and her arm, indicating I should try and touch her there. This she repelled and began another sequence. After that the dance just took over. As a finale I put my arm around her shoulder, without of course touching, and she did not resist, kissing me on the cheek instead. The crowd laughed and cheered. It was quite an introduction to Chaumarga.

Chaumarga is a village of 4,000 people divided into seven wards in the administrative district or *kabupaten* of Tabanan. Bali is constituted of eight districts, each corresponding to one of the eight Balinese rajadoms in place at the end of the eighteenth century. In order of precedence they are Klungkung (where the Javanese Hindu rulers first settled), Badung, Tabanan, Bulelang, Jembrana, Bangli, Karangasem and Gianyar.

Chaumarga village is governed by a council, *krama desa*, representing both the community as a whole and the ancestral spirits of the villagers. In former times the council owned farmland on behalf of the villagers, but now individual ownership is the norm. The *desa* makes all decisions regarding the affairs of the village including the organisation of festivals, the administration of justice, and the allocation of duties.

Like the village as a whole, the family compounds within the village and wards are each surrounded by their own wall consisting of a number of buildings each equivalent to a single room. Each compound is entered by a gateway over a raised doorstep of stone. Behind the gate is a wall, necessitating a turn to the right or the left to gain entry. The wall is there to prevent evil spirits from entering—spirits only travel in straight lines (something I also learned from the Aborigines).

I went to bed late that night to the sounds of dogs barking and woke up early in the morning to the sounds of cocks crowing—daily life here begins at daybreak with family prayers and ablutions. This was followed by a breakfast of spiced bananas, boiled eggs, tapioca, banana fritters, and coffee, all grown locally. Then we bathed at the public springs in cool mountain water, woman to one side, men to the other.

After bathing, Ketut's father left for his garden plot, which he tended on weekends, and his mother left for the market while Ketut showed me around the village. Chaumarga contains two main temples, or really three in two. In one of them, the left side is for Brahman and the right side for Shiva. In addition, there is a separate temple for Vishnu. These temples are overseen by Brahmanas in the village, but there is no Kshatriya caste. The local line ended when the last Kshatriya family had no sons; they adopted a boy, but he moved to Kuta. A Sudra family was looking after their house and temple.

Ketut said that I was the first foreign guest in the village and that the headman had already sent word that I was to visit him—with my passport. I could see that Ketut was a little uneasy about this, and I worried that I might get his family into trouble. (As it turned out the meeting was uneventful, as the headman, too, treated me as an honoured guest.)

We left the village and made our way across a stream and up to the terraced rice field above the village. We were headed for Ketut's uncle's land. I noticed that some of the fields were marked with a pole from which hung a piece of cloth. I asked Ketut about this, and he said these fields were ready for planting. The sign meant "Leave alone." In other fields oxen ploughed the soft ground. As if to anticipate my question, Ketut said, "We tried using small tractors in the rice fields, but they couldn't plough as deep as oxen and the rice wasn't so good, so we went back to oxen." Another example of tradition beating modernisation. At his uncle's home we were treated to another feast of Balinese food—boiled rice flavoured with chilli pepper sauce, fresh coconut, oranges, and coffee. The visitor be forewarned, most Balinese food—meats such as chicken and duck, fish, vegetables such as corn, marrow and beans, and even prepared fruits such as bananas, papaya, and pineapple—is hot, very hot. If you believe that sweating makes you healthy, then Bali is the place for you.

The next day was Kleywun day, the day for making burnt offerings to the *butakala* or "bad gods" so that when they arrived they wouldn't make trouble. They came every five days. Every offering, Ketut said, has three ingredients: fire to take the prayer to the gods, water to purify, and flowers for fragrance which concentrates the mind. The offering itself is a five–colour ball of rice (red, white, black, yellow, and grey). An offering is made in every room in the house, outside on the road, and in the driveway. Ketut was not telling me this just to educate me, he was telling me so that I would participate as a member of the household. He also told me about "shaking hands." The Balinese don't. That's the Indonesian way; the Balinese hold their hands together in the praying position and bow slightly to one another. However, one may shake with one hand while grasping the wrist with the other if one wants to indicate deference or issue an apology. I was expected to behave accordingly in the village.

The next morning Ketut had to return to Kuta and he dropped me off at Sanur beach for the day. It wasn't a good idea as I was in village mode, and Sanur is where the rich tourists hang out in Bali. So I decided to find myself a relatively isolated stretch of beach, away from the hotels, and just sit out the day. I don't know why, but I began to feel my losses again, Iain's death, my marriage break–up, my estrangement from Graeme, and I began to get very mad at myself and, I guess, at life in general. Then all of a sudden I was aware of someone standing beside me. It was a middle–aged man wearing a turban, and he was real. I must have been so preoccupied I didn't see him coming. He looked at me and said, "Why are you so angry?"

"I'm not angry," I barked back.

"I was walking along the beach and I saw your aura," he said. "It was orange."

I calmed down and he sat beside me. He was a Sikh from India and he was about to return home. Would I like my fortune told? I suppose so. Would I write down my favourite flower and colour on a piece of paper and hide it in my hand? Blue and a rose. "Blue and a rose," he said to me asking to see what I had written. Then he did the same thing with my birth date and the number of children I had and got those right too. He told me that the pain in my life would eventually end and that October would be a good month for me, but things would not really turn around for another three years. I would live to be 96. Then he got up and left, and like the fortune teller in Singapore simply said, "Remember." (I know it is easy to make predictions "happen," but that October was when I rediscovered my daughter's love, and three years later in 1992 I again revisited the

Aborigines.)

Back at Chaumarga that evening Ketut took me to a *gamelan* rehearsal (photo 15). There are two styles of playing depending on two kinds of orchestra, *angklung* and *gong*. An *angklung* orchestra utilises four pieces of metal, as they put it, a *gong* orchestra 10. Ketut's village could only afford a four–piece. The four are *tarrong pong*, a round percussion instrument with a small hub in the centre played with two sticks; *gangsa*, a 10–stick xylophone; *kampur*, a stand up gong; and *ja:gogan*, a five–stick xylophone with wide bars. These instruments are accompanied by a drum, *kandang*, and a flute, *suling*. Only men play. Women dance.

Gamelan music represents the spiritual world and reproduces its laws of form and motion epitomised by the separate but interlocking rhythms of the music. To the Balinese, as to my Aboriginal friends, the sounding of music and the uttering of words has an intrinsic power which does not depend on the meaning of the sounds emitted. This power (*lango*) transcends *maya* and in fact brings order to the world if it is emitted and heard correctly. It is this power which, in a sense, causes a *gamelan* performance, a dance, a play, to take the form it does and which impresses itself on an audience. In a *wayang* puppet play, for instance, the text is sounded to the audiences in a language most do not understand and then is commented upon by a translator. The sounding is not something waiting to be translated but has a significance of its own independently of the meaning which, in any event, is subject to interpretation by both translator and audience not to mention the puppeteer.

Listening to the *gamelan* orchestra that evening brought to mind streams flowing into a river. But which are the streams, which is the river? No conductor directs the flow, no score guides it, and yet there is order to the flow. Different rhythms are discernible, but each seems somehow to submerge into and then emerge from every other to maintain the flow at a constant rate. The music sweeps you up and carries you along, but at the same time you feel caught in an eternal moment that cycles and recycles forever.

Though money is in general use in the village, labour is usually exchanged for labour or produce for produce, based on the principle of interdependence of specialisations, mine for you, yours for me.

Some raise chickens, others plant gardens, some are artisans, and others are healers. Well, since I produced nothing nor had any particular skill to offer for their hospitality at least I could perform hard manual labour. I let this be known to Ketut's father, and his reaction somewhat startled me. Why would a professor want to do manual labour? And I remembered caste. Being a professor was akin to being a Brahmana and the Brahmanas did no manual labour at all. In Bali this is the job of the Sudra caste. However, when I insisted that the exercise would do me good, they acquiesced. I was given a hoe and cycle and taken up to the family plot where they grew vanilla and papaya. My job was to dig pits for compost then cut the grass around it and throw it in. I did this for about two hours in the so–called cool of the morning and discovered firsthand why everyone took most of the afternoon off. I was exhausted from the heat and humidity. I think they sensed my plight because they did not ask me to return with them later in the afternoon. After a few days, though, my stamina built up and I was able to follow their daily routine.

One thing I learned by watching Ketut's father was to let the hoe, rather than myself, do the work. By balancing it in your hands a certain way and raising it to a certain height the hoe makes almost as much of an impression in the ground as if you had forced it down with your muscles. The advantage is that you use less energy and can keep working for a much longer period. I also learned how attached the Balinese are to cleanliness. At the end of the working day all implements were taken down to a nearby stream and scrubbed until they looked almost brand new. It was the same with everything in the village—houses inside and out, temples, the market, and especially the people themselves.

One of my most memorable experiences came when we stumbled across a festival late one night at the nearby village of Budigu (photo 16). As we approached the village we noticed the flickering of candles against the surrounding darkness, and I asked Ketut what was going on. It was a festival for Lord Shiva, he said, at Pura Dalam Budiga temple, one held everywhere in Bali every 210 days. As the 210 days are counted from the date the temple in question was completed, it's a different 210 day cycle for each temple in the vicinity and therefore there's a constant stream of Shiva festivals going on. What drew my attention, though, was not just the candlelight but that the events were taking place around a huge banyan tree which lay on its side on the ground. The tree, Ketut said, had fallen to the ground on January the 31st last year and levelled the actual temple building. This was the day before a very special date in the Hindu calendar, February 1, "when good rises up and evil falls down." The villagers had taken this as a sign that the spirits of the temple and the nearby cemetery were not happy that they had allowed the old temple to fall into disrepair. They wanted a new one, and the villagers were now busily constructing it.

In the flickering night people seemed as spirits, moving in and out of the shadows with their offerings, appearing and disappearing in and out of the entranceway to a makeshift shrine. There was an atmosphere of sacredness in the air, enhanced by the sounds of *gamelan* emanating from who knows where in the darkness. Ketut was not allowed to enter the shrine because this was not his village, but I was led inside to pay my respects and leave an offering of flowers which had been given to me by a woman outside. At this festival there was no dancing at midnight as normally marked the conclusion. This was not only because the temple was not yet completed, but also because the villagers sensed that the *barong* spirits did not want it. When the time came to enact a complete performance, the *barong* would let the villagers "know."

My most memorable experience of Chaumarga and Bali, however, came a week later, just before I was to leave for Kuta and home. In preparation, I was instructed by Ketut in the Balinese manner of prayer. Every festival or ceremony, he said, begins by summoning the spirits to the temple or shrine and then "washing" them (*mulasti*) in the form of an effigy or statue (*lingga*) brought to the temple or shrine for the purpose. The water is then set aside until the end of the ceremony by which time it has absorbed a great deal of power. Everyone in turn then sprinkles some of it three times on their hair to clean the brain, three times on their mouth to clean the body inside, and three times on the face to clean the eyes, face, and speech. When you pray at a temple or shrine, first you utter an "excuse me" to get the spirits' attention, then you offer flowers or flower petals to the gods of the place and to the spirits of the family. Then you make obeisance without flowers to say thank you and good–bye. This last part is called *ngyad*. When a priest says "thank you" at the end, he also asks for the care of the village.

The next day Ketut told me he was going to take me to a special place where no foreigner had ever been before. It was in an isolated part of the rice paddies some distance from his home. Before we left we prepared a special thanksgiving offering of flowers and food, and r1000 for the headman of the temple (*pumanku*)—not a priest, Ketut was quick to point out. The headman was a Sudra not a Brahmana whose line had been entrusted with the care of this particular temple from time immemorial. We drove south into the countryside to just where I am not exactly sure. I began to doze off in the heat when I suddenly had this very clear image of Iain. I was awake enough to see him kind of reflected in the window and I felt at peace.

We stopped on a side road somewhere and headed out through the rice fields on foot. There was no path except the one trodden by the farmers around the edge of the paddies. Then we came to a small ravine and began to descend toward the valley below. Below to our left I could see a small building, basically just a room. I thought this was it, but it was only the hut of the headman who had come from his village to meet us for the occasion. He was introduced as Imadi Kumbu. He lived in the village of Budigal where we had been a few nights before and came here for festivals when he may stay for two or three days.

Imadi then took us down to another level and a cave whose mouth had been shorn up with bricks and fashioned into a pool fed from springs deep inside (photo 17). We left our offerings on the wall of the pool and made our way down to another level where a stream of water gushed from a pipe in the rock. We were to wash and cleanse ourselves before making the offering. Then we made our way back up to the cave and joined the custodian in prayer according to the manner outlined by Ketut. Then Ketut opened the offering bundle, took out two boiled eggs, and placed them in the pool. I had thought these were for our lunch! Suddenly two shapes appeared out of the cave and glided through the water toward the eggs. It gave me quite a start and Ketut settled me. These were holy eels (*belut*) and this was a healing temple. People came mainly to cure skin rashes and sores. When people touch eels in the fields, said Ketut, they contract skin diseases, but here the eels cure skin diseases. There's another twist too. The eels coexist with "five different colours of fish" and with crayfish, which constitute their regular diet in the rice fields. Here the eels don't eat them. The fish are thought to be reincarnations of people cured of skin diseases who wish to make *karma* by healing others and so return as humans.

After the offering we did have our lunch back up at the hut, consisting of the food we had brought that we did not feed to the eels. Then we headed home. On the way I told Ketut of the vision I had of Iain on the way to the temple and how I still felt his loss. I told him that he had helped me in a way he could not have imagined. He asked me to say a prayer of thanks to his family spirits for bringing me here and to bless his parents' home. To him I had received a power and I could bestow it on someone else.

While we were away at the eel temple, the police had come to Ketut's parents' home to check on "the foreigner" staying in the village. Meeting the village headman had been enough as far as the villagers were concerned, but not the police. I would have to travel to the police station at Marga, sign in, and surrender my passport until I left. This bothered me as did the fact that I might have got Ketut's family into trouble. So the next day we went to sign the forms and give them a departure date. Ketut said that the Indonesian government didn't want tourists wandering into the villages because they wanted them spending their money in the hotels and tourist haunts where they had their fingers in the pot. Under the circumstances, I said, it would be best if I returned to Kuta. He agreed.

My last night was spent at a special *gamelan* performance where the last piece of the evening was given to me as a remembrance of my time in Chaumarga.

*   *   *   *

I should have known. In my absence I had been bumped off my return flight to Jakarta and had to pay an official bribe money to get my seat back. I felt sorry for the Balinese who had to suffer the "Indonesian way of life" all the time.

*   *   *   *

August 22nd, 1989: I received the news last night after returning from Bali. John Lokko died in his room at the rectory in Toronto while he was taking a nap. There had been no warning. He had just returned from his summer posting in Edmonton and, according to his friends, was in particularly good spirits. I hadn't seen him since he and Francis had driven me back to the monastery. About 5 o'clock that Friday afternoon, exhausted by a long interview on Aborigines for the C.B.C., I was about to lie down when I felt this sudden surge of energy. John came suddenly to mind. Then the energy faded. A kinder, gentler, person you could not imagine. Like Iain, an old soul.

6

INDIA

Bali had calmed me emotionally and whetted my appetite intellectually. The source of Balinese culture was India and I now resolved to take up an offer made to me in 1988 but which I had turned down. Dipankar Gupta had been visiting the University of Toronto from Jawaharlal Nehru University in Delhi (J.N.U.) and had asked if I would be interested in working in India. He had put me in touch with a colleague at J.N.U., Harjit Singh, who annually took a group of postgraduate students in Geography to Ladakh in north–east Jammu and Kashmir for one month on a study tour, and he had invited me to join them. Even so, I hadn't. In the fall of 1989 after returning from Bali I wrote to Harjit and asked him if I could accompany his party the following summer. He replied that a visit to Ladakh was "not advisable at the moment because of very serious political disturbances there."

Ladakh is in the northeast corner of the state of Jammu and Kashmir and Jammu and Kashmir is coveted by both India and Pakistan, not to mention of strategic importance to Afghanistan, Russia and China. When the British left India in 1947, they partitioned the country to allow for the separate Muslim states of Pakistan in the west and Bangladesh in the east (originally conceived as one state). Muslims fled India to Pakistan amidst persecution and violence, and the two countries have been at loggerheads with each other and over Jammu and Kashmir ever since. India was given control over Jammu and Kashmir at partition, but on the understanding that a referendum eventually be held to determine whether it would be part of India or independent. That referendum never came.

Jammu and Kashmir is the only Indian state with a majority Muslim population. An independence movement had sprung up in the state led by the Jammu–Kashmir Liberation Front (JKLF) and the extremist Jamaat–e–Islaami (JEI) which is fundamentalist Muslim and pro annexation to Pakistan. By 1989 some 43 militant organisations were pressing for change in Jammu and Kashmir. Pakistan was waiting in the wings for an excuse to intervene and India was waiting for an excuse to bring in military rule. Under the circumstances Harjit had to change his plans and had organised a trek for his students into northern Himachal Pradesh on this side of the Jammu and Kashmir border. We would move from Dalhousie in the west to Keylang in the east and pass from a Hindu region through a tribal to a Buddhist one. The trip would give me the opportunity to experience firsthand a more ancient form of Hinduism than I had encountered in Bali.

I arrived in Delhi on June 1st, 1990, reached Harjit's place at 1:30 a.m., was up at 7:30 the next morning to reconnoitre with the students.

"What shape am I in compared to last year?" I wrote in my diary.

"The pain is gone. Sometimes a slight emptiness of the heart but nothing like before. Focusing almost entirely on Michelle has helped. She is very strong and is a stabilising force. Last year at this time I felt the losses more acutely and had trouble going to Singapore on my own. The year before my parents had to push me on the 'plane to Darwin. The ups and downs have levelled off, though the stress came back at the end of term what with classes, taxes and the like. That's when I seek companionship."

One thing that was worrying me, though, was the very real possibility that Michelle and Graeme would be moving to British Columbia. That would be like losing Iain all over again.

I woke up that first morning in Delhi to scorching, dry, heat with the temperature already in the 30s and the news of pending disaster. The Kashmir issue was reaching boiling point, there was trouble in the Punjab, and both the Indian and Pakistani armies had been placed on redalert. At 4 p.m. we were boarding a train to Pathankot on the Punjabi–Himachal Pradesh border and heading right into it. There would be police checks on the train, and I, at least, might be turned back. As a precaution Harjit told me to take an upper berth that night and keep my back to the aisle should the police board.

For the moment, though, it was 9 o'clock Sunday morning and time for an episode of the Mahabharata on television. The TV series, in sixty–some episodes, was attracting the largest audience in Indian television history. Harjit and the students who had arrived at his home—and myself—sat glued to the screen.

My first impression of India, aside from the heat, was crowds and squalor. First in and around the station, then on the train and finally along the tracks and in the countryside as we passed through. I had not expected to see people squatting near the tracks defecating in full public view. It couldn't just be the crowded conditions and the lack of public facilities, I told myself. People don't do this in China, which is even more overpopulated than India. Harjit told me that in fact, public toilet facilities were often available, but people didn't use them. He thought it might have something to do with the Hindu concept of "outside" or public space as profane and "inside" or private space as sacred. Enter the home of the poorest villager, he said, and you will find it immaculate. However, these are the very people you see in the fields. Even if on a very different scale, it reminded me of the "American way" of private affluence and public squalor.

I slept only sporadically on my upper berth which consisted of a plank with no bedding or pillow. Not that I needed bedding. It was excruciatingly hot and all of it concentrated near the ceiling where I just happened to be located. Harjit was right about the police. Just inside the Punjabi border they boarded the train and inspected all the carriages but without noticing me. At Pathankot the police and military were everywhere. Just the day before, Punjabi separatists had killed a revenue officer, and Indian security forces had killed an insurgent and captured 14 others. The separatists wanted their own Sikh state and the more militant among them wanted to force the local Hindus out. Many had already left.

The Sikhs form a minority in India, but there are some 15 million of them and they are concentrated in this part of the country. Their religion is neither Muslim nor Hindu but a kind of accommodation between them based on the teachings of Guru Nanak (1469–1539). God is a He but is formless, invisible, and transcendent, as in Islam, but He also exists in the human heart; one looks inward to find Him. God is also an expression of the sacred syllable OM as in the Hindu tradition. OM is the soundform or Nada Brahmana that many branches of Hinduism see as at the source of creation. Sikhism rejects the Hindu caste system, but the nine gurus who succeeded Nanak over the next two centuries were of the Kshatriya caste; so was Nanak. On the whole, Sikhs are also wealthier than the vast majority of Indians, and their lands in the Punjab are also more productive than most of the lands in India. Moreover, they have a strong military tradition and were recruited by the British to defend colonial interests in India. Most Indians would as soon flee from them as fight them.

Dalhousie to Sathroundi

At Pathankot we boarded a bus to Dalhousie, further to the north in the state of Himachal Pradesh where our trek would begin and, again, I was ordered to keep low and look the other way whenever we passed through a check point. Our accommodation was at Gandichok (photo 19), near the town itself. That's when it all caught up with me—the lack of sleep, the change in climate and diet. Exhaustion overtook me, a well of grief swelled inside me, and my body erupted. Harjit fed me glucose and I slept from 3 in the afternoon until 5:30 the next morning, waking briefly to force down a small helping of rice flavoured with dahl (legumes), potato, and cucumber. Thankfully, I woke refreshed to cool air and a view of snow–capped peaks in the far distance. We were in view of the Pir Panjal range of the Lesser Himalayas.

We would remain in the vicinity of Dalhousie for two days to acclimatise before leaving for parts east—and up. Delhi to Dalhousie had been a trip of 351 miles (565 km.) from sea level to 7,069 ft. (2,150 m.). From here we would steadily climb until we reached 15,748 ft. (4,800 m.) as we crossed the Sach Pass, and then we would descend to the 6,500 ft. (2,000 m.) range as we made our way to Keylang and Manali, before returning to Delhi. In all, we would cover over 900 miles (1,500 km.). Though only about 100 miles (170 km.) of the journey was on foot, it was the straight up and down part—the part where we were most likely to run into difficulties. In the valleys, travelling between towns, we took the local buses, though these trips too were not without their heart–stopping moments.

We were 37 in all, including four supervisors (myself, Harjit, Kamal Chinoy, Chinta Kapur, two cooks, and 31 students, 21 of whom were women. With the exception of two Muslim male students, all of them were upper caste Brahmanas or Kshatriyas. The two cooks were Brahmanas, though from a poor area in the mountains. I asked Harjit "why Brahmanas?" and he said that Hindus believe that a person who cooks food infuses the food with some of their spiritual essence—their *karma*. This is why Brahmanas cook for Brahmanas, and this is why

Hindus in the other twice–born castes prefer their food cooked by Brahmanas.

The food itself was basically a new experience for me. Hot, but not as hot as in Bali, lots of rice, lots of egg curry (spiced with onion, ginger, garlic, tomato, turmeric, coriander, and salt), lots of *chenna*, lots and lots of *dahl*, as well as *chapati*, *puri* (fried chapati), *paranta* (semi fried) and *roti* breads. Occasionally a bit of chicken or mutton would be thrown in, but only when available in the local area. All but two of the students were Hindu and vegetarian—at least up to a point. Most ate no meat but did eat eggs; some ate no meat only on Tuesdays. The two Muslim students ate meat, but not on Fridays; and the meat they ate had to be bled while the animal still lived to conform to Muslim law.

On June 7th we were off to Khajiar. We walked without our back–packs which went ahead by bus. It was part of the acclimatisation process. But the stroll was anything but leisurely for me. The students wanted to know about their counterparts in my country. Did they have arranged marriages? When did they get married? Did they have careers? For some of them, marriages had already been arranged to men they barely knew. They expected to be married as soon as the husband–to–be was gainfully employed, and they themselves didn't expect to have a career. When I told them it wasn't that way at all with us, they weren't so much envious as felt it necessary to defend their own ways. Their parents will check the man's character, his family background, his prospects—everything—before they agree. That way there is no risk for her. It's better than trusting to emotion. Infatuations come and go and can easily be mistaken for love. Why not grow into love with someone? In any event, marriage is a relationship between families, not just two individuals. Hinduism is about renouncing, not seeking, worldly pleasures.

Despite these insistences, the questions continued unabated. Did young women in my country have sex before marriage?

"Yes."

"Well, since I don't know what I'm missing, it doesn't bother me."

However, even at this early point in the trip, one could feel the sexual tension in the air as the men and women of the group found themselves in closer and closer proximity, something quite impossible in the city. It expressed itself in the form of joking relationships at the hostel—teasing, put–down humour, flirtation. Harjit was well aware of this development and was worried for two reasons: out–of–control hormones in the mountains could be a very dangerous thing, and any hint of scandal on this trek, and his own reputation could be ruined.

Though I could not escape all the questions, I could escape the number of people asking. I quickened my pace to get ahead of the group, but one of the students still kept up with me. This was Sujata. Her father was Indian from Kerela and an artist, her mother Chinese. In her this combination was striking. She had listened with interest to my account of the status of women in Canada and said she would prefer a career to marriage. In India women had to accept a certain degree of subordination to men, but then she added to my surprise, "I need to be kept under control from time to time." What's more, she liked men who were protective; it made a woman feel more feminine. Well, this wouldn't go over very well in some circles back home, I thought.

Khajiar consisted of a guest house, a temple, a few houses, and a very deep pond (*khaji*) in a meadow between us and the community. Legend has it that a century and a half ago a man decided to find out how deep it really was by making a rope and lowering it down into the water. He made and lowered the rope for 12 years but it still didn't reach bottom. At this time of the season, however, the pond looked more like a puddle than a pond as it had dried back to its source, leaving the ground very marshy. It did, however, reveal the cow dung left by watering cattle during the rainy season which was being left to dry by the locals so it could be used as fuel in the winter.

We weren't the only visitors to Khajiar. Eight government officials were here from the Punjab, complete with an armed bodyguard and Sten guns and pistols of their own. They came over to see us as soon as they saw the women in our party. Harjit did his best to discourage them, but they insisted on a return visit when we were settled. Then, later in the afternoon, there was a commotion near the pond. I rushed on to the veranda of the guest house to see one of the officials with a gun in his hand walking toward a pony, obviously angry and intent on doing it harm. Harjit ushered the women indoors and told them to stay in the back room of the hotel while Kamal headed toward the official. Kamal and some of the others in his party were able to persuade him to put the gun away. However, he grabbed the pony's reigns with his left hand, picked up a stick with his right, and started beating the animal. Eventually he mounted the pony and began hitting it on the neck, then punching it. Finally he rode in circles until its legs almost gave way and then he took off across the meadow. It was sickening. Better this, though, than a dead pony, or a dead Kamal or one of the others who intervened. Later, Kamal said the man was drunk and lost his temper when he couldn't control the animal. We should stay as far away from that group as possible. Fortunately the incident was reported to the local police, and the officials were told to leave. Talking to one of the local hill people with one of the students the next day I found out how really dangerous the situation was. He said it was a local pony with whom he had shared the same water. To hunt the pony, then, was to hunt him; to hurt the pony was to hurt him; to kill the pony was to kill him. Had the police not intervened the locals would have banded together to beat up the official. Considering the armaments the officials had, though, it could have turned very ugly indeed.

Though it was not as hot as in the lowlands here (we were at 6,955 ft. or 2,120 m.) it was still in the 80s (upper 20s C), and yet none of the men in our party, except me, wore shorts, and no one took his shirt off while he was walking. I wondered why. I asked Kamal and he said it was a question of modesty. The men would be embarrassed to uncover their bodies to the women. Furthermore, one had to be careful about one's reputation amongst the people we met, even up here. I had another question for him. The women were spending upwards of two hours getting up and washing in the mornings with the result that we were always late starting the day's activities. Was this necessary? Yes it was, he replied, at least to Hindus to whom cleanliness—a component of morning prayers or *puja*—was equated with spiritual purity.

The evening before we left for Chamba I visited the local Naag Snake Temple with Suparna, another of the students. The snake is an important Hindu symbol/deity associated with Vishnu and Shiva and the snake deity here represented all the snakes that ever existed. Propitiating it would bring good luck. By the time we had paid our respects, however, it was past dark, and we arrived back at the hostel to another commotion. It seems Aslam, one of the Muslim students, had also stayed out after dark in the company of three of the women. Harjit was beside himself. It was this respectability thing again. The locals would talk and that talk could get back to the university or the students' parents. I wasn't sure exactly how, but I didn't argue. The students were divided on the issue. Some thought it silly to have to behave up here as you did in Delhi and wanted the freedom; others didn't want romances developing and so supported Harjit's new curfew rules.

As for me? Whatever Harjit wanted to do was O.K. by me.

The next day we were off to Chamba, a fair–sized town to the east where we would catch a bus further north. By the time we reached our destination, though, my system was in turmoil—cramps, nausea, a high temperature. They called it "fever" and said it was due to over–exertion. It would pass. In the meantime, chew betel nut and sleep. The betel nut (a hard nugget that becomes fibrous after much biting and chewing) settled my stomach. I chewed it and then slept for 18 hours and awoke refreshed.

We were on our way by bus to Brahmaur, an ancient Hindu settlement, when we stopped in a village for refreshments. I took the opportunity to stretch my legs and walked ahead on the road. I turned back to admire the view and was about to continue my walk when I saw a man coming toward me with flowing white hair and a long beard dressed in a light, pink, cotton tunic and pants. Some kind of connection occurred between us, and he suddenly broke out into a broad smile. The marks on his cheeks and forehead told me he was a holy man, a *sadhu*. I bowed with my hands held in the prayer position before me only to see him hold out his hand to shake mine. We did, and he said "thank you," though I could not imagine what he was thanking me for. I raised my head to thank him in turn and froze as I looked into his eyes. They appeared at once cloudy and clear, distracted and penetrating. I felt he was looking deep inside me. I don't know why but from the look I felt like I had just met Galiyawa, an old Aboriginal friend on mine from 1969. Then he unfixed his gaze, smiled, and went on his way.

Brahmaur sits on a hillside surrounded by mountains. At its core is a temple complex whose pagodas date from the 10th or 11th centuries, but the site itself is much older. An old wooden temple on the site, dedicated to Laksana Devi the goddess of Brahmaur, was built in the seventh century, and the site as a whole is associated with the early Aryan settlement of India between 1750 and 1500 B.C.

The Aryans entered India from the north with their armies and their sacred scriptures (the Rg Veda) to conquer the local population and introduce the four varna or caste system into India. Their scriptures recount the creation of the universe from the sacrifice of a "cosmic giant" from whose mouth emerged the Brahmana caste, from whose arms the Kshatriya, from whose legs the Vaishya, and from whose feet the Sudra. The Harijan or Untouchable caste was likely the tribal hunter–gatherers they encountered whom the Aryans felt so beneath them technologically (they themselves were pastoralists and farmers) that they viewed them as something less than human beings.

In the village of Brahmaur there are 84 temples, including the five in the central complex, each dedicated to a different deity, though all are in some way related to the Gods Vishnu and Shiva. Ganesha, the elephant–headed god, for instance, is Shiva's son. One of the five main temples is dedicated to Ganesha, and I sort of adopted him as my "patron saint." Ganesha is the god of perseverance, of over–coming all obstacles, and I figured I needed all the help I could get in that area.

There were too many people milling around the temple complex during the day for me to get a real feeling for the place and it closed up at night. The only time to come would be in the early morning. It was at 7 a.m. the next day that I made my way up from the hostel just as the young guru of the temple was sensing the various shrines of the compound (photo 20). I sat down to watch, trying to be as inconspicuous as possible, though how I could manage that with my camera slung over my shoulder and my notebook in hand I wasn't entirely sure. He opened the door of the shrine before me to a life–sized image of a man seated in the lotus position. The carving looked so real I thought it was, but I dared not approach to check it out.

I watched the guru sense the other buildings and expected him to withdraw inside, but he didn't. Instead he beckoned me over and gestured that I should accompany him inside one of the buildings which turned out to be his own dwelling. Facing me on the right as I entered was a small shrine with a photo of the man I saw in the shrine. On the left was another small shrine to the temple deity. At the back of the room in the centre was a window in the form of a triangle through which the sun shone. He led me to the shrine on the left and made a mark on my forehead then sprinkled water on my cupped hands before placing sugared sweets in them, which I then used to make an offering. Then he led me to the other shrine and stepped back, indicating that I should show my respects on my own which I did. After that, he led me outside, thanked me—why, I don't know—and told me something about himself.

His name was Jay Krishin Maharaj Jelha or Primahil Maharaj. His master, Maharaj Jee—the man in the shrine—had died before his young pupil was fully instructed, so that every day after his death the young guru comes to the shrine to receive further instruction. Jelha still remains in touch with the spiritual being of his teacher and through meditation on the image is able to receive instruction just as before.

Later that evening as the sun was setting I returned to the temple complex and stood beside Jelha's house gazing out toward the mountains. And then it struck me. It was nearing the summer solstice and the sun was setting to my right in the wedge between mountainside and horizon. I realised that at solstice it would also be shining through the window of the young guru's house and illuminating the shrine on the left. My guess was that at winter solstice the sun would be setting in the wedge between the horizon and the mountainside to my left and would shine through the window to illuminate the shrine to the guru on the right. It was one of those moments of clarity that you know is just right whether you ever get to test it out or not. This was why the temple complex was located in this spot. It was kind of an observatory, a calendar. If I now imagined standing back and looking through the guru's window at the mountains outside I would gain the impression of a mandala, a symbol sacred to Hindus and Buddhists. The mountain slope on my right and the one on my left would appear to "join" at the mid–point on the base of the triangle which formed the window. This would form an inverted triangle overlapping the triangular shape of the window. I felt a sudden rush of joy and understanding. Yet no one had really taught me anything. I had just *seen*.

It was now the 14th of June and we were on the road to Bairagaar and the Sach Pass where we would climb to our highest point. All along the road, we passed small shrines, many of them containing stone *linga* or phallic symbols representing Shiva. Travellers stopped here to pray for safety and we were no exception. We had learned that there was still snow on the Sach Pass and that even the sherpa porters who plied the summer trade routes over the mountains had not yet ventured over. We would have to cross three to four miles (five to seven km.) of snow, most of it on our ascent. Would the porters we hired be willing to proceed? Should we proceed? If we did, were we up to it? Anticipating problems, Kamal and I left the trail and trekked down the valley to the village of Tirila to buy axe handles (we carried heads) and walking sticks for everyone. The locals we met were bemused that we would try crossing the Pass at this time of year with a party of women.

The area we were entering was densely forested and full of wild life including leopards and bears. As well, there were cobras about. Two tribal peoples lived here, the Gaddi and the Gujar. The Gaddi were small–scale farmers, the Gujar were pastoral nomads. The Gaddi were Hindu, the Gujar Muslim. The latter came with their cattle to graze the slopes in the winter, returning to their lowland pastures near Pathankot just before the snows came. The Gaddi were here year–round. The Gaddi provided the Gujar with vegetables, and the Gujar provided the Gaddi with milk products in turn.

The students were beginning to open up more and more as we trekked along. Many weren't quite so inexperienced as they had first led me to believe. Some smoked and drank alcohol which is officially forbidden to both Hindus and Muslims. Some had boyfriends/girlfriends their parents didn't know about. Some had even slept with them, and some wouldn't mind having a boyfriend/girlfriend on this trip.

The problem with the porters was immediate. Of the 12 we hired for the crossing only nine showed up which meant the ones we had hired were overloaded. They were not happy. Harjit feared more would leave before we reached the Pass. Fortunately we were invited to camp overnight at a place called Ranikot where a group of Gujar nomads were settled in for the summer (photo 21). Two of them, Abdul who spoke English, and his brother Hanif, agreed to guide us over the Pass. This seemed to pacify the porters somewhat as they knew the Gujar to be expert mountaineers.

Up until this point in the trek I had been wearing my running shoes, but thought it wise now to switch to my hiking boots, a pair of "Hi–tecs" I had bought at Mountain Coop in Toronto. Imagine my shock when I discovered that one shoe was a full size smaller than the other and that it would not fit my foot without completely cramping my toes. I had not worn them after trying them on in the store and whoever packed them had packed two different sizes. I was going to have to manage the snow and ice with my runners, an unsettling prospect indeed.

Abdul Hamid Khan had been studying English at school and hoped to attend university, so that our arrival proved fortuitous for him. Harjit and Kamal promised to help him apply to J.N.U. as a member of a Scheduled Caste for which a certain number of places were reserved each year. Scheduled Castes are basically tribal people, most of whom are illiterate. A few like Abdul, however, were able to squeeze through and could be of considerable help to their people if they were able to enter the professions. Abdul wished to join the public service of Himachal Pradesh and work for the betterment of the Gujar. They were currently being taxed for moving their cattle up to the mountains and there was pressure from the government on them to stay in Pathankot year round. In the mountains they were treated as separatist sympathisers who would fraternise with their compatriots across the border in Kashmir. Abdul thought that he might be able to change these attitudes if he worked in the government.

The trek to Sathroundi at the base of the Sach Pass was a premonition of things to come. As I put it in my diary,

"We went on a hell of a hike across ice fields and over cervices opening down to valleys of snow and ice (photo 22). Finally, when we were all exhausted from the climb we were led on a 'short cut' by Abdul which to a Gujar means 'straight up' rather than round about. The 'short cut' ended in a single log bridge across an icy mountain stream which most of us literally crawled across. I was beginning to discover my physical limits. I couldn't have gone another step further after reaching Sathroundi."

Sathroundi consisted of a rude stone guest house, two *dhabas* or tea stalls and a few tents and primitive stone huts for the local Nepalese who serviced the porters and travellers who would soon be coming over the passes. I had my cup of tea in one of the tents, watched attentively by two young children who simply couldn't take their eyes off me. I think I was the first European they had ever seen. I reached into my rucksack and gave each of them a pen. Instead of writing, though, one of them took both pens and began to use them as tapping sticks to beat out a rhythm. Their mother laughed and so did I. So I took one of the pens and showed them how it could write, then gave them both some paper and left them to it.

The conversation in the tent was not encouraging. A ghurka mountaineer had come across the Pass from the other side a few days before but had fallen and his body still lay in one of the crevices. This news triggered a debate between Harjit and the Nepalese about whether we should be crossing at all. One thing was for sure. We would only cross on a clear day.

The Sach Pass and Beyond
The next day was cloudy with some rain, but by afternoon things began to dry up and the locals said the next morning would definitely be clear. However, if we wanted to be sure of getting across before the weather changed we would have to leave at daybreak and be at the summit of the Pass by noon in order to be down the other side by mid–afternoon. That was the most likely time for an abrupt change in the weather. Given our track record getting going in the mornings I knew we were in trouble and told Harjit so. We were encouraged that the first donkey train of the season would be leaving before us to make the crossing. Our porters would accompany them. Harjit appointed Abdul and me to be the lead party as he knew we would be first up in the morning and had experience in snow and ice. We were to take three of the students with us.

I went to bed that night more than apprehensive. The Nepalese were taking bets as to how many of our party would be killed during the crossing.

Abdul and I were up and ready by daybreak. Unfortunately our travelling companions were not. Nor were the rest of the students. It was 8 o'clock before we left in the lead and we could see that the rest of the party would be some time following. In any event, the sky was a brilliant blue and not a cloud was to be seen. The view was magnificent. We quickened our pace and despite the late start reached the summit of the Pass at 12:30. Harjit had instructed us to wait there until everyone had ascended. He would be in the middle of the pack and Kamal and Abdul's brother Hanif would bring up the rear to help stragglers. By about 1:30 the others finally joined us on the Pass, but, of course, had to rest. Abdul joined the students in prayer at a small shrine at the site (photo 23) and there were photos to be taken and stories to tell. The skies were still clear and the warnings that had been issued were forgotten. It wasn't until about 2 that we started down.

We descended about 600 feet (200 m.) when the sky in front of us suddenly grew dark, and the wind began to blow. In an instant we were in a snowstorm. The line of students inching down the slope froze. Aslam started yelling at them to get moving. Panic set in. One of the women lost her footing and slid down the slope. Fortunately her rucksack caught in the snow and she ploughed to a stop 300 feet (100 m.) below. Hanif literally raced down the slope to retrieve her.

Meanwhile I moved back up the slope to the first student in line who happened to be Sujata and took her hand. I told her to look straight at me and just begin walking. She did and the line began to move forward. Then I left Sujata with the others and returned to Abdul and the lead party as we slowly moved ahead. It soon became obvious that we had made a mistake. We should all have turned back to the Pass where at least there was shelter. The snow was suddenly joined by hail. Visibility shrank to just a few metres. We found a rock face and tried to shelter, but it was useless. We were getting soaked and it was below freezing. We would have to continue our descent. By now the trail trodden by the mule train and the porters earlier in the morning had disappeared from view. There was no sign of anyone behind us, and we weren't sure which direction would take us safely down. Abdul told me to take Mira and go in one direction and he would take the other two and go in the other. When one of us found a way down he would shout.

The route I had taken became steeper and steeper but there was no sign of a trail or the valley below. I had Mira by the left hand when all of a sudden I took a step forward with my right foot and there was no ground beneath it. Now it was my turn to freeze. "Don't move," I said to Mira. I turned and looked down and my foot was hanging in thin air. Another step or lose my balance, and it was certain death far below. Mira knew it too and tightened her grip. There was this moment of awareness between us and she said, "If we die, thank you for getting me this far." For some reason the "we" in her comment seemed funny. All she had to do was let go of me and she at least would be safe. I laughed. "Just keep your balance," I said, "and lean back so I can shift my weight." She did and I managed to pull myself back from the chasm. Then I said, "Pull hard and fall down on your back." As she did I fell back myself and we were both on solid ground. We crept back up the slope and then headed across hoping to somehow locate Abdul. Soon we heard talking and with a shout discovered Abdul and his charges huddled behind the stone foundation of a derelict hut. Better still, the snow and sleet had changed to rain. We would not freeze to death here. We took what plastic bags we had and fashioned them into a canopy which we asked the students to hold over their heads. Abdul had found the trail nearby and he wanted them to remain here while we descended to the *dhaba* in the valley where the porters would be waiting. We would come back with help. There was still no sign of the rest of the group behind us and we feared the worst.

So off we went. The trail was narrow, in some parts dangerous, but it was a trail. As Abdul vanished in the late afternoon shadows before me, leaving me to manage on my own, I realised I had put my backpack back on and it weighed a ton. And I was completely exhausted. I felt I couldn't take another step. All I wanted to do was lay down and sleep. It would have been so easy. However, I knew I had to go on. So I took off my rucksack and left it on the trail. But as I moved forward I slipped on the ice and almost went over the edge. I just sat there unable to move. Then I thought of Iain, and I looked up into the sky and said out loud. "Iain, give me strength." Then I felt a warmth in the area of my navel and it began to spread throughout my body. I stood up with a sudden surge of energy, picked up my backpack and started walking down the mountainside.

On the way down I passed the donkey train, shivering on the slope. One of them was laying down—dead. They had run into trouble too, despite the earlier start. And then I saw a group of men coming toward me. It was some of our porters. I knew Abdul had reached the base. By the time I reached the *dhaba*, Abdul had already dried off, had some tea, and was on his way back to help. I did the same and we spent most of the night leading the students down to safety. It was fortunate indeed that Kamal and Hanif had remained in the rear, behind the students. In the darkness, one of the students, Moana, had fallen down the slope among the rocks and disappeared from view. Hanif, though, had managed to climb down and find her. Somehow she had slid between the rocks and had suffered only some minor cuts and bruises. He carried her on his back up the slope. How he managed to find her in the dark without getting himself into difficulty no one was quite sure. We chalked it up to experience. However, there was no doubt that she owed him her life.

There was a great deal of bravery on the slopes that night, but there was also a dark side. When Abdul reached the *dhaba* at the base and asked the local Nepalese for help, they refused unless they were paid a considerable amount of money. When Abdul objected, all they said was, "All right, we'll bring back the frozen bodies in the morning." So Abdul turned to our porters who themselves had suffered through part of the same storm while laden with our supplies. They returned to the mountain with him without a murmur. It's worth mentioning the head porter by name—Sardari Lal—as he sought no gain and received little credit, certainly no "bonus," for what he and his fellows did that night. Like Hanif they literally carried the students down on their backs.

We all fell asleep in a heap in the tent, propriety blown to the wind, men holding women, women holding men or each other.

The next morning we awoke late and refreshed. The first thing I did was locate Sardari Lal and give him my Hi–tek boots. The smaller one fit him perfectly and the other he could wear comfortably with a woollen sock. It was as if I had bought him a car! He had never had proper boots before. His whole yearly income from portering amounted to r12,000 or about $360. It was a hard life and his body would eventually break down. However, he loved the mountains and he would never leave it for work elsewhere.

We would rest this day and depart for Kilar in the morning where the porters would leave us. Conversation during the day focused on "fate." Was it or wasn't it? Why did we get caught in the storm? Why did we nearly die? It wasn't getting up late in the morning. It wasn't inexperience. It was the will of the Gods. Consensus concluded that Abdul had offended the Hindu mountain deities by showing disrespect at the shrine on the Pass. It wasn't just that he was Muslim, it was also that he had been singing and joking at the shrine. Poor Abdul. All he had done was get them safely over the Pass and down the mountain, and now he was not only being blamed but also shunned. Nor was there anyone to say good–bye to the porters when they left early in the morning a few days later. I felt badly for them and told Sardari so as they left, but they seemed to take it all in stride as the way things work in India. Who can really understand the way things work in India where there is so much suffering and, at times, so little compassion. We left the *dhaba* at the base of the Pass only to find that Anandita had been robbed the night before, likely by the Nepalese who had refused to help on the mountain. Suffering, I thought, bred compassion, but I could see now that it also laid bare one's vulnerability, and there were those who would take advantage of this—and not just in India. Maybe some people just lose their soul during their lifetime. I'd hate to think a person could be born without one.

We arrived in Kilar to a hero's welcome. Word had spread through the valley about a group of city folk who had miraculously escaped death on the Pass. The miracle to the locals, though, was that we were primarily a group of upper caste young women from Delhi whom they thought to be soft, pampered, and incapable of strenuous physical activity. We were met on the way in by people wanting to carry our bags or touch us or offer us tea. When I took a shower at the cistern near our campground it was standing room only on the road above me.

The next day I found a small out–of–the–way stream and just let my body and mind relax. The drone–of the stream began to break up into distinct pitches which formed into complex harmonies and flowed past me with an almost melodic cadence. I dozed off and as I did I had a dream. Iain was playing in the grass at the farm. I asked him what should I do? He said, "Go back." His face somehow seemed much older.

I had to go back to where I belonged. These trips overseas the last couple of years were my work all right, but they were also a way to escape the loneliness of the summers when the University term ended and my regular visits with Michelle gave way to summer holidays and her time at camp. Toronto was no place to be alone in the summer and I had given up my home near Perth and I seemed unable to return to the Aborigines. So I travelled. It was time to go home.

The Pangi Valley was cut off and isolated for all but a few months of the year. The locals were tribals outside the caste system and visitors like ourselves were rare. The government, however, did have a presence here in the form of the District Officer. The incumbent just happened to be a graduate of J.N.U. and Harjit thought that he might be able to help us out with supplies. He was in for a shock.

The evening of June 23 we were invited to the D.O.'s place for mutton dinner. This was going to be a real treat after a steady diet of rice and dahl over the past few weeks. Instead of mutton, though, we got vegetables. The D.O. apologised and explained what had happened. He had ordered his cut from the local butcher, but when he sent someone to pick it up, there was no mutton to be found. It had just "disappeared," the butcher said. So in retaliation the D.O. immediately ordered his shop closed. By now I had picked up enough local information to know that very little meat was available here. When a goat was killed, its meat was sold in less than an hour. No one had much food, and the butcher's had gone to those more in need than us. Nonplussed, the D.O. said he would do better next time and offered to accompany us as we trekked to Cherry Bungalow and Rooli.

Two days later when we reached Cherry Bungalow we were invited to the D.O.'s quarters again. To make up for the loss of the mutton, he had ordered a 5 1/2 pound (2.5 kg.) chicken from the local *dhaba* owner. Dinner began with a serving of spiced potatoes which was followed by egg and vegetable dishes. Then came the chicken—two small plates of neck and wing parts. And that was it. The D.O. asked the server where was the rest of it and the answer came back, "It's all gone." The *dhaba* owner had given the best parts to the locals. The D.O. was beside himself, but there was nothing he could do. His official position gave him considerable powers but he had no way of exercising them on people who had no respect whatsoever for his position or whatever person occupied it. There was but one police station in the whole region, and the police were preoccupied with what was happening across the border in Kashmir. In any event, there was no law and order problem because the locals were a law unto themselves, and as far as I could tell, it was a just, Aboriginal–like, law. Take from those who have much and don't really need it and give to those who have little and do.

From Cherry Bungalow it was by foot to Puurthi and from there by truck to Rooli where we would board a bus to Keylang and the Buddhist region of Himachal–Pradesh. Harjit insisted that our backpacks travel with us on the truck as he feared that the porters we had hired in Kilar might run off with them when they reached Rooli. We were now on the edge of a lucrative black–market trade route extending from here through Tibet and all the way to China. However, there was nothing in the porters' behaviour that indicated treachery. They had happily walked on minus their loads and came to our farewell party the last night at Rooli, joining in the festivities with songs and dances of their own.

Keylang to Manali

Keylang proved to be a brief but interesting stop–over on our way to Jaspa further to the east where the students were to conduct a survey of the area. Kamal and I would take the opportunity to visit a nearby Buddhist monastery. My appetite had been whetted by the sight of Tibetan monks in Keylang and the *chorten* and *mane* I had seen along the road.

A *chorten* is a kind of shrine composed of a stone base on which is a small tower with an opening on one side containing a *mantra* or prayer written on a scroll. These *chorten* are usually located on the outskirts of villages or near *gompas* or Buddhist monasteries for the purpose of warding off evil spirits, though travellers often stop and pray at them. *Mane* are walls of stones each carved or painted with a *mantra*. The stones are placed by the roadside as an offering from people who have been blessed with good fortune of some kind. Once in place they are believed to give travellers good luck as they pass by.

To steal one of these stones, as some tourists have done, is to cause someone's death, though not necessarily that of the thief. I was told a story of one American tourist who took a stone home as a souvenir and had so much misfortune befall her that she returned with it to the spot where she had found it. Some of these walls reach 2 miles (3 km.) in length.

Gautama the Buddha was born to a royal Kshatriya family in Lumbini in what is now Nepal circa 563 B.C. He died in 483 B.C. Though he married and had a son, Rahul, he grew increasingly dissatisfied with the affluent life of the court and ventured outside to discover a world of suffering from which he had been shielded. He renounced his old life for one of extreme poverty and set about seeking Enlightenment. However, extreme asceticism proved as blind a path as extreme affluence. One day while meditating under a *pipal* or fig tree Buddha received enlightenment and entered Nirvana while still remaining in a living body. Afterwards he taught in and around Sarnath in north–east India and after his death his teachings, collections of sayings known as *piteka*, were written down into what we now know as Buddhist Scriptures. Ironically, many of the sayings attributed to Buddha warn of the danger of relying on the instructions of texts over the lessons of experience in the quest for Enlightenment. He also warned of the questing itself being an impediment to Enlightenment. The mind must loosen itself from all attachments including the wish to loosen itself from all attachments.

Unlike Jesus, Gautama is not worshipped as a person, as a particular human being, but as the incarnation of Buddhahood, a kind of quality which manifests itself from time to time in human history.

Buddhism recognises no enduring soul which survives after death. However, it does recognise souls which are unable to progress beyond the human cycle of rebirth to gain entry into Buddhahood. Somewhat reminiscent of Hinduism in this aspect at least, the soul is conceived as a bundle of urges and desires which must be eliminated in each successive rebirth before passing into a state of nonbeing or Nirvana where the soul ceases to exist. Buddhism rejects the caste system with its notion of fixed stages of rebirth as well as any notion of a Creator. Though Buddhism's early converts were Hindus, Hinduism as a tradition rejects Buddhism as a more complete revelation, though many Hindus regard Gautama as an incarnation of the god Vishnu.

By the sixth century A.D. Buddhism had virtually disappeared from India, though it had spread to China (Mahayana Buddhism) and south–east Asia (Hinayana Buddhism). In the seventh century it reached Tibet through the Chinese–Nepalese Buddhist wives of king Srong–Sen–Gam–Po. The Tibetan version spilled back into India in the Himalayan region of Ladakh and Leh and in Lahul–Spiti near to where we were now located.

A common core of teachings lies at the heart of Buddhism whether Hinayana or Mahayana. The Four Noble Truths state that life is suffering, suffering has a cause, that cause can be extinguished, and that extinguishment comes by following the Eightfold Path. The Eightfold Path is right faith, right resolve, right speech, right action, right living, right effort, right thought, right self–concentration. The substance of what is right in each case is set down in specific teachings.

Basically, suffering can be exterminated by a complete cessation of desire for four things: for being, for lust and desire, for pleasure and for power. As I remarked in my reading of Buddha's teachings in Singapore, this is to be effected by "detachment"—the apprehension of people and things independently of your own interest in them. This achieved, according to Buddha, compassion results and suffering ends.

A Buddhist community is referred to as a *sangha* and the most devoted of *sangha* are the monasteries. Here the monks, both men and women, practice detachment and the cessation of desire in isolation from the larger Buddhist or secular society. A monk's entire life is to be devoted to this endeavour to the exclusion of labour of any kind. For his or her sustenance a monk is dependent on the generosity of the layperson.

The monastery we were to visit near Jaspa was Gamu, the umbrella monastery for some seven *gompa* in the region. On the way up to Gamu, we made detours to two small *gompa* but found them to be locked up and without a resident monk. Along the way we stopped for lunch, and I was introduced to Tibetan food, a plate of *momos* or small dumplings filled with meat that one dips in hot sauce, and a bowl of *thukpa*, noodle, vegetable, and meat soup.

The *lama* or head monk, at Gamu was named Dhashi and he had been here for 25 years. The original monastery, he said, had been destroyed by an avalanche and a new one built on the same site in the 1970s. The site owes its origins, so legend goes, to the *lama* of Ladakh who had thrown seeds into the air from his abode in the mountains and where each one landed and germinated a *gompa* was built. I was surprised to learn that Dhashi had privately owned land nearby on which he grew potatoes, barley, and peas. Dhashi said that this was a poor area whose Buddhist population could barely afford the upkeep of the *gompa*, let alone support himself and the monks. They were forced to supplement donations by growing food of their own. The Buddhist population was declining as many young people were converting to Hinduism and the monasteries were occasionally subject to vandalism, including the theft at Gamu of its main deity, Tjurgi Lapa, Protector of Buddhism. He had regarded this as an omen.

On June 29th we retraced our steps to Keylang and then headed south to Manali, the last stop on our journey. Arriving in Manali was like landing in the lap of luxury—modern hotels, good restaurants, shopping. Then a strange thing happened. All the lamenting during our trek that we were missing the Mahabharata series and the World Cup of soccer on television suddenly ended. T.V.s were available at the hotel, but no one seemed to care. It was as if the lament was a way of keeping in touch with "civilisation" while we were out in the wilds, but now that we were back, there was no further need. I often find myself doing much the same thing when I travel overseas, trying to find a North American newspaper to check the baseball or hockey results, something I seldom do when I'm at home. It provides a kind of continuity in discontinuous circumstances.

Early on the morning of the 30th, I left the hotel and headed for the Buddhist section of the city. When I reached Himachal Nyinmapa temple the front door was open, and I could hear a monk chanting his *mantras* inside. I took my shoes off and entered, pausing lest he should show any signs of annoyance in which case I would leave. However, he turned his head and caught my eye, beckoning me to sit opposite him on a mat provided for another monk. In his right hand he held a small cymbal, which he struck with a stick in time to the rhythm of his chant. I sat there as best I could in half lotus position and let the repetitiveness of his voice and the striking of the cymbal transport me. It was the most relaxing experience I'd had in the past month.

Manali is also a Hindu centre, boasting a temple associated with the Mahabharata epic. Hidimba temple was built in 1553 to honour the Pandava clan, which came here in exile and where Bima met and married the demoness Hidimba. A somewhat more gory sight of significance is a nearby sacred tree containing the spirit of a sheep-eating god which demands animal sacrifice in return for answering the prayers of the people who come there. The carcasses hang from the branches.

Manali was also where we reconnected with the news on Kashmir. On June 29th separatists killed the Assistant Deputy Commissioner of the capital, Srinigar. The thing was, he was a Muslim, a Mr. Aziz Ahmed Khan. The Student Liberation Front who claimed responsibility for the killing labelled him "an Indian agent and a cruel officer." The SLF said that Kashmir belonged to Kashmiris, and all outsiders would be killed if they did not leave the valley. Indian security forces countered that this and other organisations were agents of the Pakistani government and did not represent the majority of Kashmiris. Severe measures would be taken to ensure the security of the area. (On July 5th the Governor promulgated the Jammu and Kashmir Disturbed Areas Act, 1990, giving the police widespread powers of search and seizure and the right to fire on and kill "a person who is indulging in any act which may result in serious breach of public order.") Harjit was wise to have cancelled his trek through the region. What was happening there made our adventure on the Sach Pass seem like a Sunday School picnic.

*　　*　　*　　*

July 2nd was Graeme's birthday, and I hoped he had received the card I sent. Canada seemed like a long, long, way away indeed, at this point.

*　　*　　*　　*

After gorging ourselves for two days in Manali on everything from trout to Tandoori chicken, we left for Delhi just as the monsoonal rains were arriving. Sixteen hours and a gruelling bus ride in the heat and humidity later, we arrived and said our good-byes.

July 4th was the day of Mohammed's enlightenment and an

Indian national holiday in honour of the Muslim faith. It was to be a day celebrating the spirit of reconciliation between Hindus and Muslims, but judging by the events transpiring in Kashmir this day, it was more like a day of mourning. Accusations and counter accusations flew back and forth in the media and spilled over on to the streets. Partition had produced a separation but without interdependence. Neither Muslims nor Hindus knew how to use their differences to bind one to the other as Aborigines in Australia had. Theirs was the legacy of thinking in terms of mutual exclusions—my faith for me and yours for you with no giving from one to the other. In this they were not alone in the world.

On July 7th the Indian government proclaimed the Armed Forces Special Powers Ordinance, 1990, which further expanded police powers in Kashmir. I felt sorry for the Gujar nomads we had encountered before crossing the Sach Pass who were trying to live peacefully in both worlds and up to now, at least, had seemed to succeed. Abdul's hopes to enter the Himachal Pradesh civil service would now certainly be dashed, but at least he could continue his studies at J.N.U. with help from Kamal and Harjit. I had taken his mailing address and planned to keep in touch with him and help in any way I could. A couple of hundred Canadian dollars would carry him through the entire academic year. After graduating, who knew but that circumstances might change. I had learned a great deal to do with my studies on this trek through north India, but perhaps the most satisfying thing of all was knowing that you could make a difference in someone's life, however small it might seem at the time, whether it was helping someone out of physical danger, giving your boots to a porter, or supporting a student through school.

*　　　*　　　*　　　*

I used to think I could change the world—simply using the force of ideas. Now I knew that ideas alone can change very little. Ideas were only a guide to experience and without the experience of, say, suffering, detachment, compassion, and renunciation nothing in my or anyone else's behaviour would really change. You had to reach the core of a person's being to effect change and you couldn't do this just by convincing them on some intellectual point. To do this, you must truly feel a need in them as if it were your own, and move to fulfil it without regards to your own. Do this, and they will be moved to you—and what this act represents—in turn.

  * * * *

I'm back in Canada travelling on the train from Smiths Falls to Toronto again. I have my Walkman with me, and as we leave Kingston station I put on Beethoven's Fifth Symphony. This performance, I note, is by the Israel Philharmonic hosting the Berlin Philharmonic, Zubin Mehta, conducting. The programme notes speak of the concert as symbolically building a bridge (between former enemies) "to a world that is pure and good." I think of this possibility for Hindus and Muslims, relax and let the music transport me.

I watch the passing countryside, the trees, their leaves emerging from their buds and bursting into new life. The rhythm of the train, the music, the changing landscape, begin to mesh. Things appear ahead and disappear behind. Square cut fields, stone houses, golf courses. The train slows to the second movement. The waterfalls at Napanee. They vanish. The limestone court house. A flag. A blue water tower. An old stone station. The majesty of Old Ontario. Expressed in the music. We pick up speed. Ploughed fields enclosed in fences. A pond. Fence posts speed by. The train quickens to the music. Repetition. Resounding chords. A stand of pines. A stand of poplars. Square–cut fields. A stone house again. A quiet theme. The tempo of the trains slows. Then a swelling of sound and pulsating rhythms as the train picks up speed. The music is back where it began with the original theme. Open fields. A bridge. Cedars. Lake Ontario in the distance through a clearing. I glance back. Everything left behind. Going where? Remnants of an orchard. Gone in a blink. A sailboat on a trailer. The music grows soft. Ribbons of steel appear beside us. We must be approaching a town. Past Belleville station. The train quickens to the music. A silver water tower. A Church spire. Frame houses. All left behind. Suddenly the highway. Cars beside us, left behind. The music becomes serene as we move back into the countryside. I hear laughter in the seat behind me. The music quickens and returns to its original theme. A crow swoops down to the ground. Two people in a field. Maples bursting, sugaring done. A junk heap of old cars. The music swells. A factory. Dissonance. We slow to a halt. Trenton Junction. Thirty–four minutes and thirty–four seconds, Beethoven's Fifth, from Kingston to Trenton Junction. This is how it will always measure for me.

Detour to New Zealand

In 1992 I returned to Australia, first to give a paper at a conference at the University of Melbourne, and then to travel to Groote Eylandt to talk to the Aborigines about coming back early the following year to continue my work. On the way I stopped in New Zealand to visit Ellen and my mother's sister's family who lived just outside Aukland. Here is my diary account of my encounter with Ellen:

June 23

On the 'plane to Vancouver–Auckland. Have decided not to read Ellen's notes again but wait until I see her so she can first recount what happened to her. Am sorry to leave Michelle behind. My dad is OK but tiring easily. Anything that touches him at all and the spot turns black and blue (he is in the first stages of leukaemia). Easy weekend in Perth with Beverley and Michelle. They seem to get along great. That has been the most difficult—being in Perth with someone other than Ruth. Michelle takes it all in stride. She is growing up rapidly and brilliantly. Beverley persists, despite me, and I'm not sure how it will eventually work out. I'm beginning to relax and enjoy, or, as Michelle would put it, "Go with the flow."

June 25

6:30 a.m. The 'plane landed and just before it touched down they started playing the theme from the film "Ghost" on the intercom. What a weird coincidence considering I phoned Ellen when I arrived and am seeing her tomorrow.

June 26

At my cousin's. Slept from 7:30 p.m. to 1 a.m. Woke to music in my head—Enya of all things—then slept until 6 when (cousin) John turned on the news before heading off to work. I'm feeling very relaxed and peaceful. Thought I wouldn't be as I'm seeing Ellen today. Just relax and take what comes.

Ellen I knew from the photo she sent me. She's even more down to earth than I expected. Just a regular person leading a regular life with no pretensions. It turns out that Ellen is originally from Perth in West Australia. She was actually there the year I arrived to do a PhD. Perhaps we had already crossed paths.

Ellen says it seems appropriate that she's an Aboriginal working with the Maori and I'm a Canadian working with Aborigines. She's right: a part of one difference in another.

She says she has always had the ability to see. She thought other people saw what she saw, like the auras around trees—some coloured, some not—some trees hot, others cold (as Aborigines I worked with also saw them). She was surprised to learn growing up that not everyone saw what she did. When she receives messages they come in the form of images not words. She then uses words to communicate them.

In the afternoon we drive up to an old Maori fortification, high on a hill. On the way down we stop at a stand of trees. Ellen says for me to stand with my back to one of the redwoods and let my mind go free. I do and just listen to the birds without thinking about anything at all. Then I begin to notice my back is warm all the way up and down the spine. I go over to a pine tree and do the same thing, but nothing happens. I now know at least one sense in which some trees are hot and others cold.

Ellen is certainly not my image of a New Age visionary. She's too down to earth, not airy fairy enough; she smokes, she drinks, and she eats meat.

In a shop to get some books. Ellen sees some plants outside. "I wonder what she's got that I haven't," she says out loud to herself and picks a few stems to replant without so much as a by–your–leave to the proprietor. Well, they *are* outside and, true to Aboriginal logic, if someone has what she has not she is entitled to it.

I notice she has trouble driving. She seems quite nervous and I ask her about it. She says she has trouble living in the real world of others and keeps away from it as much as possible.

I also notice that she seems tired. I asked her about this. She says I am drawing on her energy and it is very hard on her. I should learn to control that. I should invoke God, the universe, or whatever power I believe in, in the morning when I get up to give me a cone of light around myself to protect me—and others—from this.

I mention Beverley to her and about starting out all over again and she says Beverley may only be with me for a short time. We talk about writing and she says the only point of it is to communicate to people how to *do* something. Not academics. They write to convince others they're right.

June 28

Had a bad dream. I was with Graeme up in some rocks, or at least high up. We were talking, and I remember he said something that hurt me. I began to cry. Then he came over and we walked down hand in hand. Suddenly Ruth was beside me on my left. I turned and looked into her face, but it didn't seem to be Ruth. She was much older and had a feline look about her. She put her arm around my shoulder, I think as an act of reconciliation and support, but I shook it off. Then I woke.

There was a moment at Ellen's yesterday when I was alone with her husband. He stopped what he was doing and just lay there on his back on the couch looking at me. We just looked at each other for some time. Then there was this kind of recognition. To me his face began to alter around the mouth, and there was this look of sweetness and age on his face. Then the recognition vanished.

I asked my cousin Margaret about the dream. She said it meant that I will be reconciled with Graeme but not with Ruth.

June 30

I am off to Dunedin to visit Eric Kolig, who teaches at the University there. We were contemporaries in Perth at the University of Western Australia. I recall something Ellen said the other day. Some people running things in the world today are really bad, but underneath people are good. You are good.

Eric, of course, wants to know what I'm doing in New Zealand. Without breaking any confidences I try to tell him more or less what has happened. I don't get very far. Before I'm really into it he stops me.
"I'm a member of the sceptics club," he says.

I tell him the only worse club to be in is that of the cynic. In both cases you begin from the premise that nothing extraordinary can happen. So, of course, it never does. He's not convinced. Nothing like what I'm describing has ever happened to him to upset his rationalism, and he doesn't think it ever will. My point exactly.

I have a dream. I am on Groote Eylandt with someone. I think it is a woman, but it might be a girl. Definitely not Ruth. I meet Gula and the other Aborigines. However, there is something unusual about them. Their hair is cropped short, they are clean shaven, and their skins are reddish blue and shining. Gula is telling me about pollution or something. There is water in the background and a vessel of some kind on it. I think, "Gula has become Christian," but he has not. He looks at the person I am with and remarks it isn't Ruth. She is kind of hidden behind someone and I can't tell who she is.

July 1st

Am back at my cousin's. Went over to Aunt Edna's to say hello and was just browsing over the mantelpiece when I saw a photo of uncle Vernon who had passed away recently. As soon as I saw it I knew it as the "look" I had seen on Walter's face at Ellen's.

July 2

Happy birthday Graeme.

Leaving New Zealand the way I had come—again to the strains of "Ghost" as the 'plane lifted off from the tarmac. I never did go through the reading I had with me with Ellen. I just see no need to revisit it.

July 21st

Last day on Groote Eylandt before returning home to Canada. Jambana Lalara said something sweet to me the other day when I showed him a photo of Iain. He said he belonged to them, was one of them, even though he'd only been there a short time. I knew that's the way Iain felt too.

6

JAPAN

Early in 1993 I returned to Groote Eylandt to continue the task of completing what I had started in Perth Western Australia back in 1968. This was my academic work with the Aborigines. I had recorded over 600 songs during mortuary and other ceremonies in 1969 and had intended to return in 1971 and realise my ambition to complete my original project of covering all aspects of their culture from kinship and social organisation, to economy, politics, and the arts. However, the politics of the Northern Territory intervened to prevent me, and so I was forced to return to Canada leaving the project unfinished. The C.M.S. missionaries on Groote Eylandt hadn't wanted us back because we were interfering with their attempts to convert the people and the government went along with the missionaries' wishes (*Return to Eden*, New York: Peter Lang Publishing, 1996, Chapter 1). My recordings had been stored away for almost 25 years, and I realised that by now almost all of the songmen I had recorded had died. I needed someone from that era to help me identify and transcribe my tapes. Only old Gula remained and on my visit in 1992 I had asked if he would help me and he agreed. My plan was to make two trips in 1993, the first with a former student, Philippe Rouja, and a second with my daughter Michelle (the girl in my dream?).

On my way to Groote Eylandt the second time I took the opportunity to visit Yuji Ueno, a PhD student of mine writing his thesis at home in Wakayama, Japan. However, I had another purpose too. I had been stimulated by my reading of *Teachings of the Buddha* in Singapore and by my brief encounter with lived Buddhism in north India in 1990 to the point where I had begun a serious study of Buddhism, in particular Zen Buddhism. Its direct, experiential, approach appealed to me, and I saw possible parallels with Aboriginal religion. I had written to Yuji beforehand to see if it would be possible to visit a Zen monastery while I was there, and he had arranged one through his wife's family. It was at Kokokuji, near Wakayama. Here is some background information.

Kokokuji Zen temple (photo 24) was founded in 1227 by Katsurayama no Gore Kagetomo as a place to repose the soul of Minamato no Sanetomo, the third Kamakura Shogun. Originally the temple was called Saihoji and belonged to the Shingon sect of Buddhism. In 1258 Kagetomo invited Shinchi Kakushin to become the temple's head priest. Kakushin changed the temple's sect affiliation, switching from the Shingon to the Rinzai sect of Zen. In 1340 Emperor Gomurakami honoured the temple with the new name of Kokokuji. The current abbot of the temple was Sougen Yamakawa (photo 25) who would introduce us to Zen practice.

Zen is about *doing* it rather than talking about it, so the most appropriate way of telling you what I learned is to take you through how I learned it. I will simply recount "what happened."

Sitting *Zazen*: Painfully

It was about half–past six and the shadows were lengthening as the setting sun disappeared behind the mountain tops to the west. Cobblestone steps rose before us and disappeared into the darkness as they swung to the left under a canopy of deciduous trees. We headed up and moved around the bend and onto a landing where a path led to another set of steps leading up to the main gate. The gate was locked so we made our way around to a building adjacent to the walled courtyard. We knocked on the door and were met by a monk dressed in a simple grey cotton tunic who bade us enter. We removed our shoes and followed him to an ante–chamber adjacent to a room furnished with a low Japanese table, a few mats and a very, to me, arresting vase of flowers on a shelf just off the floor to our left. There was something "right" about it, yet something "not right." I wasn't sure what, but it kept drawing me back.

From the ante–room we could look out onto the courtyard, a sweeping sandscape of narrow parallel furrows partitioned into squares and rectangles by stone pathways and in each patch of sand the odd tree here, the odd tree there. It was the trees that threw me off, one towards the back of one partition, another toward the front and off to the side as if deliberately trying to disturb the impression of geometrical symmetry fostered by the sand furrows. It was the same thing with the flowers in the vase. They looked as if they needed balancing on the right hand side to complete some kind of symmetry potential or implicit in the arrangement on the left hand side of the vertical plane.

As I looked out on the scene, now growing dim in the twilight, I imagined two now non-existent trees in the same relative positions as the ones that were there in front of me but facing toward me and in reversed position. I suddenly realised I had not only completed the symmetry potential in the scene but also recreated the Aboriginal view of the cosmos: If the scene as a whole were folded over on the diagonal, one side would mirror the other. In Aboriginal cosmology this is the relationship of life on "this side" of creation to afterlife on "the other side" of creation. The two "sides" are a sensed and non-sensed (under normal circumstances) dimension of the same space.

Sougen Yamakawa entered the main room to our right, knelt and bowed. We reciprocated and introduced ourselves. His smile was enigmatic. He wished to know if I preferred being called "David" or "Turner." I laughed, not quite knowing why. "David," I replied. He smiled back as if "Turner" would have done just as well. Then he and Yuji fell into Japanese to discuss the arrangements for our visit. Tonight we would sit *zazen* with the monks, and then *we* would decide if we wished to spend the whole weekend in the monastery. If we could bear it, we were welcome.

We removed our socks and left them in the ante-room and followed Sougen through the outer room and down a hall to our left, pausing as we passed a meditation hall on our right where Sougen stopped and placed his hands together in the praying position and bowed before a statue of the Buddha. We did likewise before moving on. At the end of the hall was another courtyard with a building directly in front of us and another to its right. Sougen motioned us to put on sandals—wooden platforms with rope bindings—and follow him. As we were walking he turned and explained the proper way to walk. The hands should be clasped in front with the head erect and the back straight. We were always to be mindful that we were in a holy place.

The building on the far right was the main meditation hall. We left our wooden sandals at the door, bowed, and entered. Inside was a platform constructed like a shelf along the walls around the perimeter. On the platform were prayer mats. In the middle of the room was another platform and more prayer mats so that the overall impression of the room was of two rectangles of prayer mats, one inside the other. We would sit side–by–side with another meditator. But in the meditation hall we would also face a meditator on the other side.

Stepping immediately into leather slippers at the door we moved to the platform on our right where we stood before our prayer mats and arranged them into a cushion by folding the length back on itself from back to front, leaving what would have been the final fold to extend down in front to form another cushion for the feet. Then we discarded our slippers and climbed onto the mat, sitting with our legs folded and awaiting instructions. We noticed that we were the only people there.

There were three aspects critical to meditation, Sougen said before we started. First was posture, second breathing, and third a clear mind. The tradition used to require the full lotus sitting position with both legs crossed and the feet up on opposite thighs, but this has been relaxed to allow the half–lotus. The lotus posture is necessary to achieve good balance as it realises equal pressure on all points in the body. To achieve this the back must be straight, the head erect, and the gaze slightly down. The hands are clasped in front, left in right, and rest just below the navel. At a later stage they may be left open and rest independently on the thighs. To straighten the back, one bends forward from the lotus sitting position and stretches out to raise the buttocks slightly and then leans back into position with the back erect.

During meditation one breathes in and out through the nose and concentrates on the exhalation, not the inhalation. Just before the out–breath expires one inhales but only briefly and when one exhales one does so from the energy point or *ki* point below one's navel. One should be able to feel the energy move down along one's legs and out one's toes, circling up the outside of ones body to a point just above and to the back of one's head. Then one draws it down and in on the in–breath by pushing down from one's diaphragm at the energy point. The important thing now is to establish a constant rhythm in one's breathing. One does this by counting to oneself in one's mind until one gets into a rhythm; then one stops counting.

As you sit, Sougen said to me, thoughts will pop into your mind. Don't let them. Say "stop" to yourself and keep them out. Focus instead on a scene in front of you, perhaps the mat across from you on the other platform. Don't focus too long on just one point, though. Instead, relax and expand your gaze. The whole point in meditation is to relax and keep those thoughts out.

Now we began. I shifted into half lotus but found I first had to rearrange my mat to accomplish it, raising the sitting cushion by increasing the number of folds so that I could bring my legs underneath me and take the pressure off my hips. I had never sat like this before and my muscles weren't ready for it. I managed the half lotus, but not to the extent of placing my left foot on my right thigh. I had to settle for tucking my foot between my thigh and calf. It was reasonably comfortable and Sougen came over to have a look, but not before peering down at my sandals on the floor in front of me, bending down and straightening them out. Just another little lesson before we began.

Sougen took his position about half a dozen mats away to my right and I was suddenly startled by the sharp clap of two wooden sticks. Then came the ringing of a struck bell which seemed to go on forever. I started well enough and got into some kind of rhythm with my breathing, though I couldn't quite get that "down through one's legs, out one's toes and back in through one's head" feeling. Despite myself I seemed to be breathing more with my lungs than my diaphragm. At least I didn't seem to be thinking about much else, and I managed to fix my gaze on a mat on the platform at the far side of the hall as Sougen suggested. I began to feel a bit dreamy, though there were no dreams. I don't know how long this went on, but all of a sudden I began to feel off–balance, like I was going to fall over backwards. This distracted me for a time, but I managed to regain my balance and concentration.

The light was changing on the surface of the mat I was watching as the room began to grow dark. My gaze began to widen so that I saw the whole room in front of me, almost to the point of being able to see Sougen to my right and Yuji to my left. Then I heard a movement to my left and the sound of the sticks startled me again. The bell rang in my ear. Twenty minutes had passed. It hadn't seemed that long.

We undid our legs. Apart from being a bit stiff, they seemed all right. They hadn't gone to sleep. Sougen said to relax for a few minutes, and then we would sit again. We did but I didn't really get back into the same position or mood I had achieved after regaining my balance during the first session. At the end of our second 20 minutes my feet were numb and my legs, lower back and hip ached. It is very important, I thought, to get comfortable right from the start because once one is in position one is stuck with it.

After shuffling our way out of the meditation hall we retraced our steps to the main building and went back to the ante–room. Sougen said that we were to return on Saturday about 7 p.m. and sit with the monks and the other guests. There would be three periods of meditation of 35 minutes each with five minute breaks between them. On Sunday morning we would rise with the monks at 4 a.m. and meditate after which we would help them in their labours around the monastery, then have breakfast. This would be followed by calligraphy—copying a Buddhist *sutra* written in Japanese characters—and lunch during which time we would be required to sit *seiza* for about 45 minutes and 35 minutes, respectively. This, I reflected, was *not* going to be easy!

Sougen said that he could spend more time explaining all this but it was better to just *do* it. "See you on Saturday."

Back at Yuji's I practised sitting for 40 minutes at a time in preparation for our return to Kokokuji on Saturday evening.

Arriving at the monastery we entered the administrative building, as before, shed our shoes, and proceeded to the ante–room where we were greeted by one of the monks and led directly to the main meditation hall. This was to be the three–periods–of–35–minutes–each session—after we sat in position for ten minutes waiting for Sougen to arrive. I was reasonably comfortable at the outset, but the underparts of my legs below the knees were not touching the mat and were kind of suspended above my feet. I could feel some pressure in my groin and lower back. The sticks and bell signalled the opening of the session, and I established an easy rhythm in my breathing and concentrated on the same mat as I had before, except that this time there was a layperson sitting on it.

It must have been toward the end of the period as the light was growing dim with the setting sun that I began to see the plank on the wall behind the person I was gazing at. I mean *behind* him, right through him. It came and went, but I was certain of what I saw. And then I noticed that from where I sat, I could see a whitish light along the left side of his body which slowly moved behind him like a shadow. This impression lasted until the clap of the sticks and the ring of the bell startled me out of my concentration. It was the end of the period.

We undid our feet and rested for five minutes then started again. This time, though, I didn't achieve a balanced position and my legs ached throughout. I had a brief glimpse early on of what I had seen before, but it went as my muscles began to throb and my legs shake from the tension. It seemed an eternity until the period ended, and I was able to undo myself. Sougen had said that we could leave after any of the periods if it was getting too much for us, but I was determined to see it through to the bitter end.

Right from the start of the third period my legs were shaking. It was painful to the point of agony, and I thought it would never end. I vowed when this was over I'd never sit *zazen* again. I couldn't concentrate at all and decided the only way out was to take a whack on the shoulders from Sougen on one of his patrols around the meditation hall with his wooden whacker (*kyosaku*). If a monk felt himself dozing off or unable to concentrate, it was his duty to signal the abbot to strike him. Some had been struck in earlier sessions, and it looked and sounded very painful with Sougen hitting down with both hands firmly gripping his whacker which did indeed make a sharp "whack" when it connected with the person's shoulder. However, it was the only way to find an excuse to get my legs out of the half lotus. To be whacked you had to bend forward so that you were hit just behind your shoulders and I couldn't do that in my present position. I would have a legitimate excuse to shift to a cross–footed position. So, as Sougen was passing silently by, I put my hands in the praying position and bowed slightly forward. He stopped and faced me and bowed in return, "apologising" for what he was about to do. Somehow I didn't think this was going to hurt him as much as it was going to hurt me.

I undid my legs and sat cross–ankled and bent forward, my hands still praying. Instead of immediately whacking me as he had the others, he reached forward and felt my shoulder, locating the muscle. Then he stood back and whacked me there. The pain left my legs but didn't come into my shoulders. The effect lasted for about five minutes. After that I was able to return to the half lotus position without much difficulty and at least sit without pain for the rest of the session.

Then, during the prayers at the end of the session, as I sat there with my legs unlocked in a more relaxed position, something remarkable happened. Sougen's voice deepened as he chanted the *sutras*, and all of a sudden I was hearing a high–pitched overtone inside my head. I didn't so much hear it as *feel* it "pingggging" away in my head and then right through my body. This had happened to me on one occasion before as I had listened to the didjeridu being played by Aborigines during mortuary ceremonies. Their hollow log instrument is capable of simultaneously producing a fundamental note and one or more overtones.

After the session, Yuji and I bathed in the wooden tub in the bathhouse with our fellow guests and I began to feel much better as the ache started to go away from my legs. Then we went to sleep on our mats, being careful to close the door of the guest house after Yuji read the sign outside warning visitors to beware of poisonous snakes which might slip in during the night to keep us company. Well, my adopted Aboriginal people's surname, Lalara, meant "dangerous snakes" and I reckoned that if I wasn't supposed to harm them they weren't supposed to harm me. I fell into a deep sleep.

At 4 a.m. we were awakened and taken back into the main building to the room where we had first bowed before the Buddha for morning prayers. The problem was, there were no mats, and I had to sit half lotus on the floor without being able to raise my torso above my legs. The ache in my legs vanished as Sougen was chanting and that same overtone "pingggg" reverberated in my head and through my body. This did nothing, though, to dull the pain of the two 35 minute meditation *zazen* sessions that followed in the main hall. When they finished I was more than relieved to get to work cleaning the monastery.

With one of the monks we gathered up our buckets and brushes and proceeded to the Great Hall in front of the meditation hall. This building is normally forbidden to the public. Two things strike one's attention once one is inside. One is a set of stairs at the rear leading up to what looks from a distance to be the mummified body of a man in monks' habit. The other is a very large dragon painted across the ceiling of the main chamber (photo 26).

The stairs, as we found out when we had to climb them to wash the woodwork, led to a wooden statue of the founder of Zen at Kokokuji namely Kokushi. I felt a sense of *déja vu* as if I were back at the temple in Brahmaur in India. Even up close one is still not sure it isn't a mummy. It was an honour to be asked to wash the woodwork around the statue and down the stairs and we treated it as such backing down carefully as we cleaned, making sure not to turn our backs on the statue at any point. Our overseer seemed pleased. Then it was on to scrubbing the stone floor. As we made our way toward the centre of the room our overseer stopped us and looked up to the ceiling to the dragon and clapped his hands. Out of the dragon's mouth came this eerie whining vibration, a kind of "wranggggg," which reverberated through the room. The monk smiled. This was the dragon crying, he said. It would only do so if you stood directly underneath and clapped your hands. Another "overtone" effect.

Finally it was time for breakfast—a bowl of rice and a few vegetables. For this it was required to sit *seiza*, kneeling with the buttocks resting on the heels, which proved much less difficult for me than I had feared. We were instructed not to eat directly from our vegetable bowl but to lift the bowl with our left hand and, with our right hand and chopsticks, transfer some vegetables to our rice bowl and eat from it. In other words, the integrity of each utensil and dish is respected and not allowed to "merge" with another. To put it in Aboriginal terms, each bowl "renounces" its contents to an "other." We were also instructed to leave one pickle in our vegetable bowl and when we had finished pour tea into our rice bowl, then with our chopsticks use the pickle to clean the bowl as we would the vegetable bowl after that. Then we would drink the tea and eat the pickle. Nothing was to be wasted.

After breakfast we did more cleaning in the main building and then broke for lunch—much like breakfast except more of it—before proceeding to our calligraphy exercise. Sougen prepared the ink by rubbing a solid ink stick on the base of a stone dish as he mixed in small amounts of water. He then poured it out into the small containers provided for us and we proceeded. Sougen had copied out a line from a *sutra* and he gave it to me to copy. He hadn't given any instructions except that I should sit *seiza* in order to bring my torso up over the table (photo 27).

Almost instinctively I held the bamboo brush erect with my wrist elevated, up off the table. I tried to capture the sweep of each of his brush strokes as I saw them revealed in his work, assuming that his hand had moved in the same direction as the thinning ink. I soon became wholly absorbed in the exercise and copied my line not once but twice. Then I noticed Sougen was standing behind me, watching. He didn't say anything but returned to his position at the end (not the head) of the table. After everyone had finished he came over and, through Yuji, talked to me. He said what I had done was very good and had I done this before. I said, no, I had made a number of mistakes, and pointed them out to him. He replied neither confirming nor denying what I had said, pointing out that each character had a right order of strokes in the sense that if the various components of the character were drawn in a certain sequence, the character would assume its best appearance. Some strokes had to be reversed without lifting the brush from the paper and to do this the brush had to be held almost upright. The arm and hand moved as one but with a certain flexibility, the stroke usually flowing outward, away from the body.

After calligraphy Sougen beckoned Yuji and me over and led us to the ante–room of his own chambers. He wanted to talk to us about my work with the Aborigines. First he served tea and a few sweets and then we talked, with Yuji translating.

Sougen had seen a cartoon of some kind depicting Aborigines as a primitive stone age people who fished and hunted and cooked their food without any preparation. This actually appealed to him. However, he wondered if there was more to them than this. Did they have a spiritual side? I tried to explain their notion of creation and renunciation. Yuji couldn't translate in a way that Sougen could understand which wasn't Yuji's fault. English was failing me.

Then I got an idea from breakfast and lunch. I took two of the tea cups on the table and placed a small sweet in each, then took out one sweet and placed it in the other cup. Then I took both from the other cup and placed them in the first. It was simple but Sougen instantly grasped in it the Aboriginal notion of renunciation—that the containing forms remained fixed while all the variable contents passed between them. Through Yuji Sougen drew a parallel with the Buddhist saying that "to have nothing is to have everything." In fact he said that this demonstration clarified the paradox for him. It was somewhat ironic considering that I had borrowed the demonstration from his instructions during our meals.

I told Sougen of my experience of the enforming light around the person sitting opposite me during meditation in the hall. He said the light was *ki*, a reflection of the Great Ego or Self connected to the universal Buddha. There was, however, a little ego or self—the source of selfishness—which had to be eliminated through self–discipline and meditation before one could reach the Great Ego. The Great Ego, then, was both one's own self and part of a larger cosmic reality expressed metaphorically as the Universal Buddha. I knew this Universal Buddha was not God nor any personified form and I knew that this Universal Buddha was not a mediator between some God and humankind. The actual person of Gautama the Enlightened One, unlike Jesus in the Christian tradition, as I said before, is completely irrelevant to, well, anything. Buddhas come and go in history, their role simply being to shed light on the nature of ultimate reality ("role" is not the best word here; they simply do what they do). The statues you see in Buddhist temples must not be mistaken for representations of Gautama, that particular Enlightened One. Rather they represent all the Enlightened Ones ever to appear in history and in meditating on their form one is carried to another plane of existence which is empty of any appearance at all. Hence "the Universal Buddha which is not–Buddha."

A parallel can be drawn here with the artistic representations of totemic beings one sees on Aboriginal bark paintings as well as the statues that are carved for the sacred Amunduwurrarria ceremony. These too must not be taken as real but as representations of something more fundamental whose nature can be revealed by contemplation of their forms—as they are contemplated by adults and initiates during ceremonies.

To the Aborigines, I explained, life proceeds from *Amawurrena-alawuduwarra* which is not so much a Spiritual Substance as a *force for forming* Spiritual Substance into types or *classes* of substances. However, it is not really *a* Spiritual Substance or *a* force, though naming it in the singular makes it appear so. It is rather a multiplicity of simultaneous Substances and forces. The lesser substances created out of these constitute prototypical selves which are simultaneously on the "other side" and "this side" of existence (*awarrawalya*) as well as incarnate individual selves (*amugwa*) within the parameters of a force for forming. These "types" we experience materially as different kinds of people, animals, plants or objects.

It is critical to realise that there is no original "one" of anything in the beginning or now in the Aboriginal scheme of things. "Oneness," to them, is an illusion (*maya*); difference is real.

To me there seemed an implicit oneness or all–encompassingness lingering in the background of Buddhist teachings, whether this be Buddha, Buddha Qualities, Buddhahood, or even *sunyata,* Emptiness. Ultimately in Buddhism, reality is one something—or one nothing. This is not the case in Aboriginal religion, and I attempted a demonstration by way of the experience I had of "laughing waves" with the Aborigines (page xvi).

What I saw was the illuminated presence of waveForm repeated over and over again countless times as a separate dimension over and above the flow of the waves themselves. The experience really had five levels. First was the experience of water—matter—itself as it formed into waves (as it is always doing). The second was the impression of waves as such. The third was the perception of waves as a discernible form. The fourth stage was the perception of the Form of each wave as another plane of existence over and above the water itself. Add to this scene of waveForms the dynamic of "spitting" as the Aborigines call it, the wisp of whitecap on each wave suggestive of force and motion, and the overall impression is not so much of water—matter—passing through waveForms, as of waveForm(s) expelling matter—spitting it out—one to the other. A fifth and final stage would be the Form of those Forms, a singleness of Form that defined each and every wave as a wave. However, this would be my conceptual imposition on the scene—an intellectual projection beyond the scene, not something I actually saw.

Sougen's reply to all this surprised me.

Gautama the Buddha, he said, didn't have the whole story. Had the Aborigines been taught their way of life by someone, or was it just there? He had taken my point—my demonstration with the tea cups and sweets and of the "laughing waves"—and was looking for evidence of a previous Buddha–incarnation among the Aborigines to explain how they knew what I told him. I didn't know, though the

Aboriginal people of Groote Eylandt and Bickerton Island do tell the story of Nambirrirrma who descended from the sky in the pre–European past to reconfirm the Law.

I thought I had better back–track a bit. "Aboriginal society wasn't perfect," I said. "While organised warfare was absent, they did kill people for religious transgressions. They have a lot to learn from Buddhism about not killing any living things." His reply threw me for a loop. He said you could look at that as sending someone away to come back "corrected" in a later life as someone or some*thing* else. I realised that this was the way some Aborigines might look at it. If someone died before they were fully initiated, they would come back and try again before moving on. It was but one step from here to killing them if they *couldn't* be initiated. I didn't like this line of argument, though, and told Sougen so. It could be used to justify killing for all kinds of reasons. He smiled back at me, and I knew this was the answer he, as a Buddhist monk, was really looking for. Buddhism really did have something to offer Aborigines just as Aborigines had something to offer Buddhism.

Sougen said he thought I had been to Japan before—in a previous life. He felt we had once "brushed sleeves," though not necessarily as human beings. We had, he said, one profoundly important thing in common. We both were trying to keep something very important alive for future generations until the crisis occurred which would make its relevance apparent.

I mentioned to Sougen about that overtone sound I heard in myself when he chanted. Yuji hadn't been aware of it. Sougen said that something happened to his voice during chanting that he couldn't explain. It sort of dropped and deepened, and he could feel an echoing in it. I said that it sounded like Tibetan harmonic chanting and didjeridu playing and somehow connected us together. "I told you we'd brushed sleeves before," he said.

Sitting there talking I realised that the pain in the sciatic area of my back had vanished. I had pinched a nerve a few months before leaving Canada and after physiotherapy had failed to heal it my doctor had declared it chronic. I told Sougen about this and he simply nodded and said that the pain would stay away so long as I sat properly in the *zazen* position. Then he laughed. He had seen how I was sitting in the main hall and realised I must have been in a lot of pain. "If it's pain you want, we have lots of it here," he said, laughing "You must come back for another visit."

Sitting *Zazen*: Comfortably

We accepted Sougen's invitation to return again and on July 30th arrived at Kokokuji to sit with the monks. It seemed, though, that Sougen was more in the mood to talk. We arrived at 7 p.m. but instead of going immediately to the meditation hall, he led us to the ante-room of his chambers, served us tea and picked up the conversation where it had left off on our first visit. The subject, of course, was again Zen and Aboriginal religion. At 9 we were to break for 45 minutes of *zazen* and prayers.

During our conversations Sougen wanted me to recapitulate what I had said—really demonstrated—about Aboriginal cosmology on my last visit. This time I used the metaphor of a cloud.

Creation is like a vast cloud. Here and there you can see different patches of light and shade and almost make out recognisable shapes and forms. Then rain falls, not all at once, but here and there from different parts of the cloud, splashing into the ocean below. The rain stops and the waves roll across the ocean connecting all the "places" in the water where each droplet has made an impression. Finally the sun appears and the water begins to evaporate, drawing the droplets from their respective "places" back up into the sky to reform a cloud. The patches of light and the shapes and forms implicit therein, are the archetypal forms, the rains are in the process of incarnating and the droplets are incarnations as such. The waves effect the form–expelling–content process.

Sougen picked this up immediately. He told me how people could be separated but still connected *by* space. It wasn't conventional space he was thinking of but *ma* space or "spiritual" space. You could be connected without directly communicating. For instance, one person is in Japan, another in Italy. One steps into the Pacific, the other into the Mediterranean, and the moment they do, they're connected. Both feel warm. That's how they know they're connected. They don't become "one"; they don't "share" anything, but they're not separate. He added that Zen has another saying to express right relationship: "we share the same mat." But it's still each sharing a part of one thing rather than something of each other, I said. I went back to the "sweets in the cup" demonstration I had used earlier to illustrate what I was trying to communicate. He thought for a moment and then responded: "We have a saying for that in Zen. In order to fill you first have to empty."

Zen isn't concerned with debating apparent inconsistencies in dogma or even with translating its teachings into a secular blueprint for living. Once you have experienced Enlightenment you simply behave in the appropriate manner. That's it. Zen has no interest in constructing institutions.

"But a monastery is an institution," I replied.

"Zen is just a method of attaining Enlightenment," was Sougen's final word, bringing us back to what we were here for.

I had a very good sit after our conversation. Sougen opened the shutters in the hall, and the wind wafted in bringing the scent of pines and sounds of frogs and crickets. I quickly entered into a restful state and my vision began to widen and take in the whole of the room in front of me. I began by gazing at the mats on the platform on the far side but soon began to see only the spaces *between* the mats. Sort of a "no–matform" experience. However, as soon as I was conscious of this I lost it. Still, I was startled when the bell rang to end the session and felt I could have sat much longer. Afterward, during prayers, I heard that overtone ringing in my head again. This time I could almost *see* it but it didn't quite "materialise."

Sougen mentioned how meditation can be used in healing. If you are ill with fever you meditate and imagine you have something like a block of melting butter on your head. It is very warm and it starts to drip all around your body to the tips of your toes until you are enveloped in it. Then it begins to move down off your head and upper body until only your lower body is covered. That's when you start to sweat and after sweating you are well. Sougen uses the technique in winter to keep warm in the meditation hall when there's snow on the ground outside and it is freezing cold. I told him I thought he was cheating. Zen monks are supposed to put up with such discomforts . . . .

At one point in our conversation Sougen and I both found ourselves explaining to Yuji something we were trying to explain to each other. We suddenly realised that we had understood each other perfectly well without the use of language. That "said" it all.

Sougen said that Buddha and Jesus both gave intellectual expression to the Truth so that it could be taught. He said that if I could do that for what I knew of Aboriginal culture, it would be equivalent to what Buddha and Jesus had done. I laughed. No, I retorted, what it would mean is that all the Aborigines are Buddhas and Jesuses and that I had been well taught. Anyway, as I noted at Notre Dame du Calvaire, if what Jesus and Buddha and the Aborigines know *is* really different from what was known in their times, how would anyone recognise it? Language bounds and organizes experience for us and we immediately put accounts of new experiences into old categories. In fact, the accounts of the new experiences *have* to be expressed in terms of the same old categories, else they wouldn't be new. So how can the newness be communicated? The Zen way, said Sougen, was by a direct experience, by demonstration and example. This was the way the Aborigines had taught me.

I really felt at ease at Kokokuji. Not *déjà vu*, but at peace with myself. About 11:30 p.m. we left, promising to return again.

Back at Yuji's I mentioned that it would be nice to have the experience of a Japanese tea ceremony before I left for Australia. Yuji smiled: "You already have," he replied, "each time we visited Kokokuji." The Japanese tea ceremony was Sougen serving us tea. I hadn't clicked in, thinking it to be something ritualised, compartmentalised, separate from "just drinking tea." I read up on the ceremony and then thought back to our tea times at Kokokuji.

The tea room is a special room, usually "four–and–a–half mats" in size, separate from but connected to the main dwelling. Outside is usually a small garden and a fountain or pond where the guests assemble, wash and chat before the fragrance of incense wafting from the room beckons them to enter. Entrance is by a small panel about three feet square in the wall. A painting, a scroll containing a *haiku* poem, and a flower arrangement face the guests on the opposite side as they enter. These they discuss until they hear the kettle boil and sing and tea is served. Each of the guests is served in turn and each drains his or her cup in three swallows, the host being the last to do so. The host then places the tea–making equipment before the guests for their inspection. He then offers each of them an item but retains the mixing bowl, breaking it at the conclusion of the ceremony. The point of the tea ceremony is to cleanse one's senses from contamination. The painting cleanses the sight, the flowers (or incense) the smell, the water boiling and being poured the hearing, and the tea itself the taste. Basically the above description is what happened each time we had tea with Sougen.

When we entered Sougen's ante–room, he invited us to sit *seiza* at the table but said that if this was too difficult, then to sit cross–legged. Then Sougen left the room and Yuji and I chatted about our experiences at the monastery and about the objects in the room—a pen and ink drawing of bamboo in black and white, a large urn on its right and a small flower arrangement on its left, behind which was a cylindrical vase, behind which again propped up in the left–hand corner of the alcove was a stringed instrument called a *shamisen*. We wondered about the age of the painting and commented on the simplicity of its style. My gaze was then drawn from the painting down to the flower arrangement (which seemed to complement the mural but in a way I couldn't quite pin down), then up to the vase and *shamisen* and finally to the urn and the scene as a whole, including the framed paper window on the far wall of the alcove which seemed to expand the space beyond itself.

Then Sougen re–entered the room with a bowl, a small bamboo whisk and a caddy containing powdered green tea. These he placed beside his mat and turned to what I now realised was an electric water boiler behind him to his right. He left the room and returned again with a large bowl, some jellied sweets and three drinking bowls. As we chatted and ate our sweets Sougen took the tea from the caddy and put it in a large bowl and then turned and poured in the hot water and began mixing the contents with the whisk, whipping it into a froth. All the while we carried on the conversation almost oblivious to what he was doing. Then he placed the bowl on the table and poured the contents in turn into my drinking bowl, then into Yuji's and then into his own. We drank at leisure thereafter, though I noticed that Sougen drained his cup at one swallow.

The Aboriginal renunciative logic in this is too obvious to be ignored. For one thing there is the pouring of the tea by one who has all the tea to those who have none. However, something more profound, in fact, structures the whole ceremony. The guests enter the room with nothing then become nothing with subsequent purification; they are now entitled to everything in a material sense and so receive. The host, by contrast, begins with everything and, appropriately, ends with nothing.

On August 7th Yuji and I returned to Kokokuji. Sougen was away in a nearby town officiating a funeral, and he had left instruction for us to sit with one of the other monks. This we did for about 40 minutes. When Sougen returned we sat with him for another hour but in two half–hour sessions. In between he took us for a brisk walk around the adjacent temple building to loosen up. Sougen was determined to make our sittings as easy as possible so that we would be encouraged to continue on our own.

Toward the end of the first session with the other monk, I was concentrating on the space between two mats just below a low light. The meditation hall as a whole began to grow dim and the mats began to disappear. The same thing happened about half–way through the next session as I sat with Sougen, but now there were parallel bars of light running right across the room. During the third session the bars of light became one–dimensional, and they too faded away, leaving a blank room except for a dim spot of light. Yet I felt alert and awake, more so than in any other session. Even so, when the bell sounded to end the final session, my body gave a start as if it had been dozing.

This was the first time that the experience at the end of one session carried through immediately into the experience at the beginning of the next despite the break. Was it the effect of *ma* ? When I asked Yuji about this he said, yes, you didn't withdraw your *ki* during the break but were actually continuing your meditation.

Afterwards we retired to Sougen's ante–room where we drank tea and chatted until about midnight. I had brought with me an article I had written on the Aboriginal view of creation which contained photographs of two bark paintings which I asked Sougen to interpret. I identified the animal forms depicted on one of the barks for him as Dove and Rainbow Serpent belonging to the Wurramarrba and Wurramara people, respectively. I told him that I had always wondered why in Aboriginal culture a particular species of animal or plant was attached to a particular people and another to another.

Anthropologists had lots of theories to explain why Aborigines had totems, but no one had succeeded in explaining why particular totems were attached to particular groups. Sougen thought that it didn't matter. If "spiritual nothingness" was behind each of these incarnations, including human ones, then each was really the same. In other words, to him the question was meaningless. I could almost see his point, but to my Aboriginal way of thinking and perceiving, the "spiritual nothingness" of a species or a group had a particular identity or archetypal Form, and I could not see why the shape of the Snake connected to the shape of the Wurramara people. On the other hand, if both Snakes and people originated in the same spiritual substance, whatever form it took, it only became two perceivably *different* forms at a later stage of incarnation, and Sougen was right.

It was now midnight and time to say goodnight and good–bye. On the 10th of August I was flying to Brisbane Australia.

Back at Yuji's I continued meditating each morning, but it was never quite the same as at Kokokuji. It was much harder to keep thoughts from creeping in and distracting me. My legs seemed to ache even more, though I was sitting for shorter periods. However, I did see things in illuminated, outlined, Form akin to my experience of "laughing waves" with the Aborigines and of myself on the train, and I did lose parts of the room and of people from time to time, though the experiences did not last long. Whether this was an experience of *awarrawalya* or outer–spirit or was simply "nothing at all," as Zen insisted, I was not sure. Perhaps they were both the same thing.

The therapeutic physical effects of meditation persisted: no more sciatic and back problems, no more ache in my Achilles tendon, no more stress in my shoulders, no more pain of grief in the space in my solar plexus which now seemed somehow filled, no more troubling thoughts from the past, and my energy level was higher. Though alone I did not feel lonely. I sensed that the Aborigines I know and the Zen monks I met felt the same way in the same circumstances.

Was the Zen experience the Aboriginal experience? Was the Zen experience, Buddha's experience as he gained Enlightenment? What was he enlightened about? Could it have been the event that immediately preceded the experience? After six years in the forest Buddha rejected asceticism as the path to enlightenment and came to a river where he bathed (purifying himself) and accepted a bowl of milk from the hand of Sujata, a maiden, who lived in the neighbouring village. In other words, having nothing of something he received (perhaps) everything of it from someone else (pure like himself). The renunciative significance of this may be what the whole tradition is really all about. It is recorded that the disciples who left him *because* he took the milk from the maiden returned to him after he talked to them following his Enlightenment. There was indeed much to ponder (photo 28).

*   *   *   *

The work had gone well in Australia, but it remained for me to double check all my dates on song identifications, meaning and so on back in Toronto to locate any gaps and then return to Australia to check them with Gula. This I accomplished in 1994 and 1995 (publishing the results as *Afterlife Before Genesis: Accessing the Eternal Through Australian Aboriginal Music*, New York: Peter Lang Publishing, 1999). In the course of my research into Aboriginal music, however, I learned to play the Aborigines hollow–log musical instrument, the didjeridu, my ambition being to gain sufficient proficiency in it to play for Gula while he sang and to experience what the Aborigines experienced when they played it. Well, I did, but what happened was not at all what I expected:

Aborigines told me that when they played they were capable of crossing over to the "other side" and experiencing the things going on there but without participating in them. The didjeridu and the voice together were a kind of conduit to the "other side" for one's inner spirit or *amugwa*. So when the time finally came to play with my old friend Gula, I half expected that if I went anywhere I would go into his sector of the Dreamtime, meaning his country and his places of spiritual significance following the path of the totemic being he was singing, namely Curlew. But that's not what happened. I found myself, for a moment, outside myself moving above fields and fences arranged into a checkerboard pattern of deeply rich shades of green. Definitely not the Australian outback. Then I realised, I was over the Scotch Line moving toward Perth in Canada. Almost immediately the experience ended. Of course, I reflected later, I would be where most of my spiritual stuff was located.

8

SHAWANAGA

In the summer of 1994 I brought Jabeni Lalara, one of my Aboriginal *na:ningumandjerga* (person in my own Land/People on the same generation younger than I am) over to Canada to tour Native communities in the north and gain a comparative perspective on his own people's problems dealing with Europeans and the modern state. Jabeni was the President of the Angurugu Community Government Council on Groote Eylandt at the time. In the process of visiting Shawanaga, an Ojibwa community near Parry Sound on Georgian Bay in Ontario, we were honoured with a feast and a sweat (photos 29–32) directed by a Midéwiwin shaman who was brought in specially for the purpose.

The Ojibwa are a people indigenous to what is now central Canada, and the north–central part of the U.S. between Lake Huron and Lake Superior. Their antiquity there dates at least five thousand years and their precontact population probably numbered 25,000 to 35,000 people. Before the coming of Europeans, they lived by hunting, gathering, and rice harvesting. In the winter they broke up into small groups to hunt large game—deer, moose, bear—and small game like beaver, supplemented by fish, fowl, and lichens. From spring to autumn they would come together again as a community to hunt and gather and engage in ceremonial activities. The Ojibwa gathered maple sap by slashing the tree and driving in a wooden peg to direct the liquid into bark containers. The sap was then boiled and reduced to maple sugar which could be easily transported and preserved. Summer was a time for gathering berries and wild rice, and in the fall nuts and tubers were collected and stored.

The Ojibwa were not a homogenous people, though they spoke the same language. Rather they were distinguished as Mississaugas, Bauichtigouian (Salteaux), Outchibous, Marameg, Aimkwas, Monsoni, Naquet, and others. A common identity was forged with the arrival of Europeans (first the French) in the early part of the seventeenth century. Though disease and warfare followed and took its toll on the population, as elsewhere in Native North America, the Ojibwa recovered to become the third largest Aboriginal people in North America today numbering some 50,000 in Canada and 30,000 in the U.S.

Ojibwa religion is focused on the *manitous* and the ancestors or "grandfathers." The *manitous* are spirit–beings who may be animals but who act like humans and possess far greater powers. Like humans the *manitous* possess a soul–spirit and an "aura." The most important of them are the Four Winds (who control the weather), the Underwater Manitous (who control the waters and the availability of land and sea animals), the Thunderbirds (who control animals of the air and punish moral transgressions), the Owners of Animals (below), the Windigos (frozen Cannibal Creatures) and Nanabush (also known as the Master of Life who first brought medicine to the Ojibwa). Lesser *manitous* are the Great Owl, Water Beings, Holders of the Sun and Moon, and Turtle (see Christopher Vecsey, *Traditional Ojibwa Religion and its Historical Changes*, Philadelphia: American Philosophical Society, 1983)

Owners of Animals are an interesting type. Each natural species has an Owner who can provide itself as a particular animal as game to humans or withhold itself and cause them to starve. If proper rituals regarding the animal are not performed when it is killed, not only the animal but the Owner will be offended, and it will not allow the hunter to kill another member of that species. Hence the Ojibwa treat the death of an animal in much the same way as the death of a person. The hunter apologizes to the animal and explains his need for it. The Owner is thanked for the gift and tobacco is offered.

It is important to note that *manitous* are not totems and totems are not *manitous*, though species names such as bear and wolf are the same in both cases. Totems are species selected to symbolize and differentiate Ojibwa clans which are patrilineal, exogamous (out–marrying) groups. Although totemic names are passed down through the male line of descent, they are not regarded as ancestors of the clan. Ojibwa clans vary in number from four to six depending on band and location and include Loon, Moose, Kingfisher, Beaver and Sturgeon. As Dunning (in *Social and Economic Change Among the Northern Ojibwa*, Toronto: University of Toronto Press, 1973: 83) says, the totem group or clan is "a means of identifying a stranger (*pewetayk*), if he is not known to be genealogically related." The clan system, he says (page 81) "would tend to integrate, at least very loosely, the widespread small communities."

Manitous become guardians of particular Ojibwa on the vision fast around the age of puberty and thereafter are encountered on occasions such as the sweat lodge.

Though less frequently undertaken now, the vision fast was the first major spiritual event of a person's life and, like most pursuits in the Ojibwa repertoire, it involved physical deprivation and a degree of suffering. The idea here was to be in such a state of suffering as to invoke compassion on the part of a *manitou*. If a *manitou* intervened to touch one's spirit and relieve the physical pain of fasting, it could be called upon thereafter to intervene on behalf of the initiate and save them from hunger and illness. The *manitou* encountered on the fast, then, was a lifelong guardian.

The fast usually occurred during the late fall or early spring when the child was 10 to 12 years old. As the initiate's food was slowly reduced to prepare him for the ordeal (women were regarded as having no need of a vision fast as they were naturally more spiritually endowed than males), his parents and grandparents constructed a lodge or prepared a secluded place in the forest. The initiate was painted with charcoal and placed naked on a bed of grass in the hut or secluded place, then covered again with grass. After a brief fast he was given a small amount of food and then left with no food for six to 10 days during which time a vision was expected. If it had not happened by then, some food was given and the fast was continued.

The experience expected was distinguished as a vision as compared to a dream. Dreams recounted the travels of the free soul–spirit during sleep. Visions indicated a visit from a *manitou*. In a vision, animals would first appear to the initiate in human form. Then one in particular would take the person away while changing into its true identity. This would be the initiate's personal *manitou* which would give him a new name, teach him hunting skills and a song which could be used to summon the *manitou*. Then the initiate returned to camp, saying nothing of his vision for to do so would be to summon his *manitou* for no particular purpose and perhaps incur its wrath.

After the relation with the *manitou* was established, it could be activated with the aid of the song or the *manitou* could simply reappear in subsequent visions, particularly during sweats.

Sweating with Jabeni

The principal purpose of a sweat, said Roger Jones, the assistant band chief at Shawanaga (photo 32), who had organized our visit, was healing through invocation of the *manitous* and the grandfathers. When a person was healed, said Roger, you could see a glow around them.

In the sweat lodge you call on all four corners of the world and the four directions, the most powerful being the north, the domain of bear who "can heal just about anything." The sweat we were about to experience would be a very special one because it was the first time the Shawanaga people had the four colours of the earth's peoples represented, namely red (themselves), black (Jabeni), yellow (Yuji Ueno from Japan) and white (me). In preparation for the sweat the band elders were going to do a drum ceremony for us in the morning. This involved a "teaching" with the kettle drum and pipe. The pipe—its stone shaft—was some 300 years old and the drum style they would use had recently been dreamed by an elder here.

First we were "smudged" with sage and sweet grass whose smoke we gathered in cupped hands and passed over our heart, mouth, eyes, head, and ears in turn. Then we sat in a circle, and the pipe was passed around to the beat of the drum as three songs were chanted. This continued until the fire in the pipe went out. During its third time around the circle I had the distinct impression that someone else was in the room over by the drum. After the ceremony the drum was turned over to reveal seven marks carved in a circle. These marks represented seven stones for the seven grandfathers. The teaching that followed recounted the Ojiibwa view of history as a recurring cycle of war and peace moving toward a permanent peace. At the time of first contact with Europeans the Ojibwa and other Native people had been in the cycle of war amongst themselves after an earlier period of peace but were now moving into the peaceful cycle, not only in dealings with each other but also with the peoples of the world.

Later Roger explained that the "smudging" was to cleanse all the senses because only then can you feel the presence of the spirits at the ceremony. Smoking the tobacco was a way of offering

—sacrificing—it to nature as a gift. The smoke itself was a bridge between humans and the spirit world. Water too was a bridge. The drumming was to summon the spirits of the grandfathers to the ceremony. At the end of the ceremony the pipe was turned around to face backwards to send the spirits back. A somewhat similar thing happened in Aboriginal mortuary ceremonies when the ancestral spirits were picked up on the "other side" and brought back to bear witness to the ceremony on "this side."

We slept for an hour in the afternoon and then got up to help Roger prepare the sweat lodge. In front of the lodge they had prepared a small, crescent–shaped, hill with a stone at its peak, pointing east. Though there were four doors to the lodge, only one—the one facing east—was open. A path of grass led inside. My job was to sweep the ground inside clean of pine needles—*all* the needles. Yuji's job was to sweep the ground outside. Jabeni was still asleep. No one asked us to work, no one commented on Jabeni being asleep while we did. We just did what we did without obligation or ceremony. After completing our tasks Yuji and I collected firewood while the "fire keeper" began preparing a pit outside the lodge for a fire. First he piled the wood inside the pit then placed stones inside representing "the grandfathers"—four "big grandfathers" and eight or so "little grandfathers." Each of the stones was wrapped in birch bark and the wood for the fire was built around them. It was about now that Jabeni awoke and joined us.

Preparations complete, about 8 p.m. we went back inside the house and the "director" as they called him in English arrived and prepared the water drum for the ceremony. In all there were nine of us. Before entering the lodge we were smudged and given a teaching about a boy who went to the sky to communicate with the grandfathers many years ago. He is represented by the crescent moon, in turn represented by the stone in front of the mound in front of the lodge. The little boy was given the plan of the lodge and a drum by the grandfathers before coming back to the people.

To enter the lodge we were to proceed like the sun, in a clockwise direction, around the back of the lodge, line up beside the entrance and wait to go inside. I was first in line. I took the tobacco offering and cedar needles I had with me and threw them on the fire that had been lit nearby. The fire master told me I was to represent "north" and to say my own personal name to the "director" as I entered the lodge on my knees. The "director" was seated inside to my right and I crawled to my left in a clockwise direction until I came back beside him and sat on his right. The others entered in turn. When all were seated, the "director" drummed and gave a teaching as the grandfathers—the stones—now glowing brightly were brought in from the fire outside and placed in the pit before us by the "fire master." The "director" then lit the pipe which he passed around the circle in a clockwise direction along with a rattle for each of us. Then he closed the flap to the lodge and began his songs as he poured water over the "grandfathers" to make steam for the sweat.

The sweat lasted about three hours with a short pause after about two hours "to clear the air." Over the course of the three hours everyone took the drum in turn, passing it in a clockwise direction, hit it four times and said "whatever comes into your mind." First time round, I expressed thanks for being here and the honour bestowed on us. The others mainly gave thanks for Jabeni's presence. However, as the pipe made its rounds, the Native people began to open up and soon were confessing their sufferings to those present and to the grandfathers. This ranged from problems of alcoholism to abuse and loss of loved ones and the more I listened to these heartfelt sufferings the more I felt the need to reciprocate. I told them about Iain and about losing my father in February of 1994 and asked for help in dealing with their losses. It was the same with Jabeni and Yuji. Eventually Jabeni told of the problems his people were facing and how he was at a loss to solve them, Yuji said how much he missed his family, particularly So–chan, his son, who was autistic. Sounds of approval issued from the Native people present as if the confession in itself was sufficient to effect a cure. Indeed in their terms it was—the grandfathers and the *manitous* would feel compassion for our suffering and act to alleviate it.

Once I located the beat of the song with my rattle I soon discovered I could sing with the director and the others who accompanied him, even though I did not know the words. The songs were mainly refrains which began on a high note then moved down in steps or tiers to a low note before repeating, as in Australian Aboriginal music. As with Australian music, the effect was becalming.

It must have been about halfway through the sweat because the drum was at the far end to my right when I heard what sounded like a rattlesnake behind my left shoulder. I had been sitting for a long time and concentrating on the stones as I listened to the drum and each person's blessing. Then, some time later, as the drum moved on to the person second from my right, something brushed against my right cheek. I thought it must have been Roger who was sitting next to me, but he was still. Then I had the distinct impression that my own father was in the lodge—not beside me or observable to me, just a feeling, a sense of his presence.

About 3:30 in the morning the sweat ended, and we returned to the house and talked until about 4. I told Roger about something brushing my cheek. He said a bear had come into the lodge and sat on his lap and had brushed me and a few other people, including Jabeni, which he confirmed. The little boy of the teaching and a grandfather had come in near the beginning of the sweat and were followed by a lizard which had gone to Jabeni. The lizard had told the director of a big rock under the ground that was safe so long as it remained under ground, but white people liked everything in the open—nothing under the surface. They had uncovered it. However, it must be kept below the surface because it can kill people. This, I assumed, referred to the manganese being strip–mined on Groote Eylandt which was doing irreparable harm to Aboriginal health and may have been connected to my son's cancer.

Then I told Roger of my experience hearing what I had identified as a rattlesnake and of a feeling that my father was present. I said that one of the totems (a word of Ojibwa origin) of the Lalara people—Jabeni's people with whom I was affiliated—was "dangerous snakes." He looked startled and began to question me in more detail. Then he told the others and they began conversing on their own in Ojibwa for some time. Nothing more was mentioned about the incident. I suspect they took my experience as genuine but had not seen Rattlesnake or my father enter the lodge, that is, had not experienced it themselves.

The next morning when we awoke I asked Jabeni and Yuji about their experiences in the sweat. Yuji said he had felt a lot of pain from sitting and that nothing exceptional had happened to him. Jabeni said that he had felt something brush his cheek during the sweat but did not know what it was. When I said the same thing had happened to me and Roger had told me it was Bear–spirit, Jabeni looked perplexed. Though he said nothing I think he wondered, as I did, how "spirit" could feel like "matter." While Jabeni said he appreciated the honour bestowed by holding the sweat, he did not enjoy the experience. "That sweat was killing me last night," he said, referring to his three immobile hours in the lodge. "Pain is not our (the Aboriginal) way," he added. It was interesting that throughout our trip here and further north, whereas Native leaders were always presuming similarities between their two cultures, Jabeni was always pointing out differences.

*　　*　　*　　*

It was now 1996 and four years since I had communicated with Ellen in New Zealand. As I said, in the meantime my father had died. He had spent a good part of his adult life mourning the death of my brother Roger who passed away in 1970 at the age of 26, and I had tried to fill at least part of the void by returning from Australia to live and work relatively close to home. Losing his own child was bad enough, but then to lose two grandchildren was almost more than he could bear. Though he was 84 and had lived a good and productive life, there was something tragic about my dad's death. He had maintained a stiff upper lip attitude toward his losses throughout his life, and I had never seen him cry. Not until the day they took him from home into the hospital. We sat on the couch together, and I told him I loved him. All those bottled–up emotions suddenly burst forth, and we held each other for a long time. When he recomposed himself he said to take care of my mother after he was gone—and to take care of myself.

I spent the last few days of his life with him, and even when he drifted into a coma I knew he was still aware of my presence. He died quietly and was buried beside my brother, as he had arranged before his death. I was face–to–face once again with loss. My work on Aboriginal music had kept my mind occupied for a time, and I had taken up didjeridu playing as part of my therapy, in a sense combining it with Zen meditation (the monks at Kokokuji used to sometimes meditate while playing the bamboo shakuhachi flute). My research had shown a positive correlation between playing the didjeridu and the alleviation of grief. Aborigines only played the instrument when someone died and continued playing through a mourning period which could last for months. The transcendent aspect I had experienced with Gula was part of this process, taking the player, and sometimes the audience, outside themselves. The style of playing was very much a form of chant which, as I hypothesised in the case of the Trappists, instilled in the performers a sense of form and presence beyond themselves. This appeared to produce in them a Buddhist–like sense of detachment, which contributed to the alleviation of grief. Moreover, my own playing utilising circular breathing (in and out of the same time to produce a continuous sound) had a soporific effect on my emotions and served to space out and dissipate any pain I was feeling.

However, something else was wrong besides emotional pain. At first I thought it must be a virus, but tests later indicated that my thyroid gland had failed. The reason for this was unclear, but Dr. Bernstein guessed it had been deteriorating for a number of years. The thyroid gland controls the body's metabolism, and when it goes, your energy level drops through the floor, and your cholesterol level can shoot through the ceiling. Mine did. I wrote to Kate for advice and she, in turn, wrote to Ellen. Ellen's advice (16.4.96) was to try homeopathic remedies for my thyroid and Bach Flower remedies for my general health:

1. Pine
2. Star of Bethlehem—for grief, 5 drops 5 times a day
3. Crab apple to be taken 3 drops 3 times a day
4. Bach Flower Remedies and cell salts:
   (see *Bach Flower Therapy: Theory and Practice*, by Mechthild Schaffer, and *How to Use the 12 Tissue Salts*, by Esther Chapman.)

Homeopathic medicine is based on the rather "peculiar" notion—from a "scientific" point of view—that if you take a substance that produces in you the symptoms you are experiencing and successively dilute it many, many, times so that not a molecule of the original substance remains and take the dilution, it will cure you. The assumption is that an invisible residue of the original substance remains in the dilution which works as a "positive" rather than a "negative." This residue has been identified as spirit" or "energy" by practitioners. In other words the nothing that remains is not really nothing at all but rather an invisible "charge" mirroring (+) the visible, material, charge (–) of the substance. You can see why homeopathy appealed to me (for more details on the subject see George Vithoulkas, *The Science of Homeopathy*, New Delhi: B. Jain Publishers, 1993).

My thyroid was in such a bad state, however, that a cure was impossible by any means. My homeopath in Toronto, Khem Chopra, explained that homeopathy could help borderline low cases but not complete failures. (Dr. Bernstein had also said that bio–medicine could not cure a case of thyroid failure.) However, homeopathic treatment had provided me with a kind of supplemental energy which kept me on my feet and functioning with a thyroid level so low that the test they had for it couldn't measure it. This more than impressed Dr. Bernstein.

I eventually took my doctor's advice, however, and began taking a synthesised thyroid replacement hormone, but I soon gave it up because of the side–effects I was experiencing—a kind of spaced–out feeling which did not allow me to concentrate and function adequately. Fortunately there was another product on the market, desiccated thyroid hormone, a natural product, manufactured by the Parke Davis Company in Brockville. With this treatment the spaced-out symptoms I had experienced slowly vanished. Then I had to deal with my high cholesterol level and my general health.

I employed the herbal remedies Ellen suggested, cut out red meat, milk, butter, eggs, cheese, alcohol, increased my water intake, ate more vegetables and fruit, ate more fish (particularly salmon and mackerel) and exercised on a more regular basis than I had over the past couple of years. Then I embarked on Robert Kowalski's *The 8–Week Cholesterol Cure* (New York: Harper, 1989). This consisted of 3,000 mg. of niacin and three oatbran muffins, or the equivalent in porridge, per day. The 3,000 mg. of niacin takes some building up to and I began with 100 mg. doses three times a day and worked my way up to a full dose over the course of a month. Within six months my cholesterol level had fallen from 10–something to 4–something. Then I cut back to 1,000 mg. of niacin and one or two muffins a day. My cholesterol level remained more or less the same.

It was a wakeup call. I realised I had been working overtime on spirit to the detriment of my body. All aspects of one's being must be brought simultaneously into balance—spirit, body, emotions—and a continual effort must be made to keep them in balance. We shouldn't think of healing as a piecemeal activity, brought to bear only when for some reason we are not well. We should think of healing in the same way we think of well–being, as something to be continually realised. Music, meditation, a balanced diet, exercise, loving relationships which sustain us when we are not well also help to maintain us in a constant state of wellness and thus to prevent unwellness from occurring.

You in all your aspects are in a constant state of change and every change brings about an imbalance in the whole, for however brief a period before an equilibrium is re–achieved. Sometimes, however, the changes are so severe and the consequences so traumatic that drastic intervention may be necessary. That intervention, as in the case of cancer or depression, may in some cases cause worse problems than the original ailment. By maintaining a constant balance in all aspects of your life, however, you reduce the chance of major trauma in any one sector. Then, if crisis does come, whether emotional, physical or spiritual, you are better prepared to handle it. As we all know, though, this is very difficult to do in today's fast–paced world. However, we should not give up trying.

Knowing then what I know now and following my own instructions, I would have been better prepared to handle Iain's death and the other losses that accompanied it and probably could have re–balanced myself more quickly and avoided the physical breakdowns that followed. I hope that by recounting to you what I have learned, that you will be better prepared than I was to deal with crisis.

PART III

YIRRALANGWA, OUR SPIRITS LIVE

DALHOUSIE LAKE

Back at my cottage on Dalhousie Lake (photo 33) finishing this book, I reflected on the *kinds* of experiences that had redirected my life over the past decade or so. Some of these experiences could be termed "aesthetic" with a view to the spiritual such as of "laughing waves" and "robeForm." Others were spiritual with a view to the aesthetic—for instance, seeing myself on the seat on the train and viewing the landscape below me while playing the didjeridu with Gula. Still other experiences were spiritual as such. On the one hand were my experiences of *someone else* outside myself: of Iain three times, of my father at the sweat, and the "nothingnesses" of the meditators in Kokokuji Zen Temple. On the other hand were my experiences of *myself* outside myself: on the train to Smiths Falls when I had my "revelation," that night in my room at Trinity College as I tried to reach Iain, and as I was playing the didjeridu with Gula in Australia.

The other things I have recounted—dreams, *déja vu*, even visions—seem to me experiences inside oneself and I must admit I have not nearly the same confidence in the understanding they reveal as I do to the things I experience outside myself (assuming those of myself outside myself are "outside" and not inside experiences). However, since I have not cultivated an ability to remember most of my dreams, I admit to lacking experience in this area.

Three questions are raised by the above experiences. One is the question of "spirit," another is that of "revelation," and a third is that of the role of both—and anything else—in "being well."

Spirit

The Aboriginal rendering of "The Spirit Lives" would be "*angarra amugwa.*" *Angarra* means "quick," "lively," or "blow, as in wind." *Amugwa*, which I have translated as "inner–spirit," is really something more subtle than this. *Amugwa* is akin to "life force, spirit or soul," but not really. It really means the *quality* of the life force, spirit, soul and in the Aboriginal language can be used as an adjective to express this quality about things and events we would not consider spiritual. For instance, *angwurra amugwa* means "the glowingness of the fire," *augwungwa amugwa* means "the gushingness of the water." *Amugwa* is an observable quality of something (at least observable to Aborigines) that is seen or heard to activate or animate it and give it life—"life" being more broadly conceived than we normally consider it. Take the "matter" of something away and there is still some–nothing left—the essential stuff or quality called *amugwa*. *Amugwa* originates on the "other side" of existence where it returns after you die. This seems to be what I experienced of Iain after he died. At the time, though, I had no previous experience with which to compare this encounter, either in my life away from the Aborigines or in my life with them. I did not even understand this aspect of the Aboriginal experience. And what of it I did understand I categorised as their "beliefs," indicating a necessary suspension of such regarding this issue. But I did have something to go on.

In 1969 my old friend Galiyawa Wurramarrba had drawn me a representation of *amugwa* in the form of a *wurramugwa* or spirit of the dead (below). Significantly, this representation was a ceremonial one revealed only to initiates.

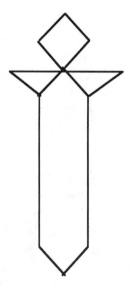

Figure 1. Galiyawa's drawing of *wurramugwa* (spirit)

What I saw on three occasions and knew was Iain resembled the lower portion of this drawing without the "arms" and "head." Of course I did not see this in my "out of body" experience on the train: all I saw then was my material body sitting on a seat albeit with an illuminated quality about it. That illuminated quality is, of course, another aspect of spirituality, namely *awarrawalya*.

Amugwa resides inside the body in a space below the navel roughly equivalent to the womb in women and a lesser space in men—the locus of *ki* in the Japanese religious tradition. *Awarrawalya*, on the other hand, lies outside the body and indeed surrounds it, being identified as "like a shadow or shade." If *amugwa* contributes the quality of "aliveness," *awarrawalya* contributes the quality of "form," that aspect of a person, animal, plant or object that causes it to be seen as a particular *type* of thing. *Awarrawalya*, then, is archetypal, generating types of things from the "other side." *Amugwa* is individual, defining the particulars within each type. The illumination I saw of myself on the train (as well as illuminated waveForm and robeForm) may be taken as *awarrawalya*, my *self* as *amugwa*. Both are comprised of *Amawurrena* or Spiritual Substance which when activated (*alawuduwarra*) is the force for forming the other two—and the matter they contain—into what they are. *Amawurrena*, in turn, is not really *a* force or substance but contains (is) a multiplicity of *possibilities*. This, then, is what "Nothing" in a generic really is: just a set of possibilities that something can happen—can form and have substance.

These three aspects of spirituality Aborigines see as working together in such a way as to enhance, or promote, life. We as humans can choose to move with them or against them. Aborigines say that in day–to–day life on "this side" people leave a spiritual "residue" in their wake as they go through life—as does all animate life (inanimate life has a residue too but, of course, it does not move anywhere). It is this spiritual residue that defines not only people's relationships to one another but also to natural species and the landscape. To go with the flow of *Amawurrena*, *awarrawalya* and *amugwa* is to act with an awareness that we are not loners but connectors who renounce a part of ourselves wherever we go and with whomever or whatever we meet as we proceed through life. That is, we unknowingly give up to others something of the *amugwa* of ourselves from the "nothingness" of our *awarrawalya* or enFormed presence. This process can be duplicated in the everyday real world of matter through the renunciation of the *things* we have to those who have them not. To Aborigines, though, this is more than just an economic transaction. To them eternal spirit "naturally" expels variable matter (in much the same way as in nature waveForms "spit out" water–matter), Spirit, then, has an inherent tendency to maintain itself in state of purity. It is what makes us *want* to give, *feel* compassion, sometimes despite ourselves .

Connectedness through this residue, then, is a natural process, one so powerful that it continues to connect us, even though we are not around in our physical bodies to make physical connection. So, when a person dies, his or her "residue" needs cleaning up, packaging, and sending over to the "other side" to join, and in a sense complete, the deceased person's spirit. If not, the spirit cannot move on into another dimension of reality, coexistent with ours but invisible (under normal circumstances) to the living. If not, the living cannot get on with their own lives and complete their own journey of understanding—to become a "proper, old, wise, person with white hair and a walking stick," having progressed through the full stages of initiation. If one dies before completing this journey, however, one's residue does not need to be cleaned up as one will immediately be reborn to try again.

However, there are those who are unable to observe and harmonise with this "flow," who do not want to give and who do not feel compassion. For them, Aborigines say, Laws have to be formulated to channel them in a renunciative direction.

Revelation

To me a revelation is a sudden, comprehensive, understanding of something you didn't know but were trying to figure out at some level of your being. It comes only when you momentarily relax your guard so that all the ways you have been trying to figure something out are somehow suspended, and you see things in an entirely different and illuminating light. Like thinking about it at a time when you don't care about thinking about it—such as when you are extremely happy about something else, or extremely sad. We recognise this as a "moment of clarity," a "breakthrough," or even a "religious experience" because the clarity often seems to come from somewhere or someone outside ourselves—which may very well be true in some sense.

My revelation on the train when I was thinking about something without thinking about it, was that life proceeds from *anti–thesis*, and ends in *plurality*—naturally in one sense, and when we let it in another. *Antithesis* is that "nothingness" in a spiritual sense—the force of *Amawurrena*—which informs and shapes us into who we are at birth as a person and in relationship to others (people and things) thereafter. *Plurality* is a ununifiable but indivisible "two," one a part of the other. The connection between *antithesis* and *plurality* is *thesis*, the materialness of one's existence that incarnates out of *antithesis* and which constitutes the renounceable stuff (or acts as the producer of the renounceable stuff) of relationship which places "a part-of-one–in–the–other." The "renounceable stuff" at issue here is not only material things but also part of your spiritual self—your vitality and energy. It was this I renounced to Iain the evening I learned he had cancer.

Plurality, then, is the result of a renunciative process.

The subtleties of a relationship of *plurality* are captured in the Aboriginal language: The term *yirralangwa* that I have translated as "our" in the chapter heading "Our Spirits Live" is misleading. We think of "our" as "we two (or more) together, more or less as one." Not the Aborigines. *Yirralangwa* means "ours but not yours" The term *Ngawgwurralangwa* also means "ours," but in the sense of "ours but not mine." What exactly does this mean in English? Well, we certainly don't have a word for it which probably means we have little experience of the kind of relationship in question. What it means is that "ours" has to be qualified as *not* meaning "shared between us" and *as* meaning "yours and not yours," "mine and not mine," both at the same time. In other words, it is "mine, but what is mine is for you," and it is "yours, but what is yours is for me." In short, renunciation.

How does one arrive at such a relationship? First by demanding what the other has to supply be it a talent, a product, a service, even though one could produce it oneself. Second by supplying what the other is demanding (even though they are demanding it because you are supplying it). In other words, what we have here is an economy based on supply and demand rather than demand and supply, as it is now. In this new economy one gives up one's own talent, product, service, to fill the "emptiness" of that in the other. Under a true supply and demand system technological and economic change become subject to a very human consideration—maintenance of people in place rather than in competition with each other. The result is technological and economic stasis (relative to what we are witnessing now)—but in a context of peaceful co-existence among people and between people and nature.

If renunciation as I have described it here is fundamental to the human condition in the sense of being at its source, then why is there selfishness and greed in the world? As we saw on the Sach Pass, not even our suffering in a life–threatening situation could prevent some hill people from taking advantage of it to rob us. Is this not fundamental to our nature too? Or is it that our spiritual nature is pure, our human nature corrupt? Is our spiritual nature renunciative and our physical nature selfish? I don't believe so.

Our physical nature originates deep inside the womb of total dependency, connected to something outside itself which it cannot see but of which it is aware and which sustains it. In this primal state of being, we have nothing and are given everything. There is no need to be selfish because the question of need does not arise. This is our first awareness. This is what we bring with us into the world. We only lose it when it is taken away, or rather when the question of need is imposed upon us (as it was on the hill people who robbed us) or when we impose it on ourselves (when we evaluate our need versus the abundance possessed by others). Where we impose need and encourage greed, then, a different form of human nature appears among us.

We certainly have that nature with us today. As Michael Ignatieff points out, we believe a competitive market will sort things out between people in a fair and just way if each simply pursues his or her self–interest to the maximum and obeys the "law" of demand and supply. We ignore the destructiveness of the process—the wastage of resources both natural and human—and lament that this is the best we can do given human nature. I don't think so. I think we force people to compete for scarce resources, compete to make a living off each other in order to survive, and when they do we say, "See, that confirms what we said about human nature being selfish and greedy."

In other words, a self–fulfilling prophecy.

As Michael Ignatieff observes, nevertheless we idealise love and post it as our utopia, albeit a utopia that seems far beyond our grasp. On the other hand, why bother even to dream about it if human nature is so set against it? I think it's because, in spite of the world we have created for ourselves, we do see examples of selfless love emerge in our lives from time to time—acts of kindness and generosity that transcend the pessimist's view. They make us stop and wonder, if just for a moment: Isn't something else possible? Is what we are, all that we can possibly be?

I am reminded of the Inuit community in northern Québec some years back that donated its entire budget for the year to the relief fund in Ethiopia. I am also reminded of our federal government who stepped in and stopped them because, they said, it wasn't really their money as most of it had come from federal funding. Some of that money, though, was my tax money, and I'm sure I'm not alone in not having minded.

I don't think the Bible is right about a lot of things, but one thing it is right about is "original sin." No, it's not Adam and Eve fornicating in the Garden of Eden. It's their attempt at isolated self-sufficiency, greed, and selfishness. They took it upon themselves to consume the fruit of their own garden, despite a warning that disastrous consequences would follow. They took it upon themselves to be self–reproducing, apart from their neighbours, despite a warning that disastrous consequences would follow. They fled before learning the secret of the Tree of Life which was that it was there not for their own use and enjoyment but rather for the benefit of someone else somewhere else. This renunciative theme crops up again later in Hebrew Scriptures, then in Christian Scriptures, as well as in aspects of Hinduism, Buddhism, and Islam, hinting of a universal insight into human "redemption" (a theme I explored in *Genesis Regained: Aboriginal Forms of Renunciation in Judeo–Christian Scriptures and Other Major Traditions*, New York: Peter Lang, 1999).

It is tempting at this point to formulate a set of institutions—rules of conduct enforceable by law—which would channel people in the direction of the flow of renunciation, whether they liked it or not. Indeed, I've formulated bits and pieces of such a blueprint from time to time in many of my publications—for instance, subdividing and federating (part–of–one–in–the–other) our political jurisdictions into mutual un–self–sufficiencies and strengthening citizenship at all levels to promote host–guest relations. Also, to give up one's abundance to those with least in the world in the spirit of infilling their emptiness, before they come to demand it. On the other hand, it may just be a matter of *taking away* those institutions that we already have that block and distort the flow of our true natures—such as taking the "competitive" out of the "competitive market system," the "adversarial" out of the "adversarial legal system"—and letting supra–human nature take its course. By "taking away" I do not just mean trying to eliminate them through political action. I also mean refusing to participate in them while they exist. I mean to go peacefully about your business but in a noncompliant way as far as these institutions are concerned.

Don't go to lawyers when you can work it out amongst yourselves, don't climb up the ladder of success on other people's backs, don't invest in exploitative enterprises, don't get legally married unless the laws of marriage are at least potentially renunciative, and so on. It seems to me the chances of electing or imposing a policy that would eliminate our present adversarial way of life are slim indeed, given the material benefits that accrue to some because of it. Elimination of what blocks the flow of renunciative potential, then, must rest on a more subtle, but no less subversive, process. As Gandhi showed, non–compliance can bring down a system as surely as any violent revolution.

The simple absence of many of our present institutions would predispose us to touch each other in heretofore unimagined ways—ways that do not require elaborate techniques and technologies to sustain them. Surely if Iain could reach me where I was, from where he was after he died, we are capable of reaching each other where we are now. We are, indeed, an untapped source of spiritual potential waiting to burst forth and transform history.

In the meantime we are going to suffer living in this world we have created. We are going to suffer trying to be different while at the same time trying to survive in this world we have created. Suffering, paradoxically, is a normal part of the renunciative life in this world. There will always be those who take advantage of openness and vulnerability, and to be renunciative is to be open and vulnerable.

Being Well

I did not enjoy being not well. However, having lived through the experience of grief and suffering I now see that it also proved to be a window of opportunity for me. I *saw* Iain after he died. I continue to experience his presence. I experienced the spiritual in a way I had not before—of someone outside myself. I did so in part because grief and pain had overwhelmed my normal, habitual, ways of thinking, feeling, and acting, to open up my sensory apparatuses to more subtle aspects of reality. Not that pain and suffering should be inflicted for this purpose (though some traditions such as the Native North American do). It's just that when it comes, do not suppress it and put it behind you. Live through it with the support of those you love and be prepared for the extraordinary in your life. On this awareness you can build.

Being well involves getting well, and getting well first means accepting that you are ill or in some way disturbed. Even before this story began I was not well. I handled Bryan's death some years earlier basically by "stiff upper lipping" it in true Anglo–Saxon fashion. Ruth and I did not really grieve the loss together, and when Iain became sick and died we paid the price for it: Two raw bundles of nervous energy flailing away in the dark. Michelle's birth proved a respite from the initial agony, but the loss had still nagged. Eventually both these and other losses combined to produce physical as well as emotional symptoms. I began to find peace and return to health, with Iain and Michelle's help, in a spiritual journey through the world religions as lived on the ground by practitioners. Meditation, music, companionship, diet—not to mention desiccated thyroid replacement hormone!—helped me back to being well.

Being well once you *are* well, to me, means living a renunciative life. Not as an absolute but as best you can while allowing some concessions to the world at large. Renunciation is something one works toward rather than something that has to be practised fully each and every time. In other words, give up what you can without leaving yourself so empty that recovery is impossible. Give up what you can but not to the point where you are taken advantage of.

Practically speaking, renunciation is the practice of acting in relation to another with his or her "emptinesses" (lacks) in mind, whether it is another person's body during love–making, another person's mind in an exchange of ideas, another person's emotions in situations demanding compassion, or another person's material needs.

Of course it is easier to live according to your principles if you are dealing with people who share the same principles. So seek out potential renouncers as your friends. Of course, the process of learning just who is, and who is not, can be a slow and painful one. You may be a long time giving someone the benefit of the doubt before you realise you are being drained and that the drainor is simply accumulating the drainage for him or herself at the expense of you, the drainee.

Living according to your principles means keeping in tune with your spiritual selves (*awarrawalya* and *amugwa*) and of those of others. You do this by what I call "Nothinging"—the exercise of clearing out the mind and cleansing the emotions so as to be receptive to the "other" in his, her, or its, own terms. This Buddhists call "detachment." It could be by Zen mediation, Hindu Yoga, Christian, Muslim, or Jewish prayer, Native sweats, or by playing an instrument such as the didjeridu or drum, by singing, or even just quiet walks in nature. Anything that takes you outside yourself.

Part and parcel of being in tune with yourself spiritually is maintaining your sensory apparatuses in a fit state. This means clearing your bodies of toxic substances, chemical residues, alcohol, and the like. This is what enables you to "see," "hear," "feel," beyond your ego–self, perhaps to penetrate the veil of appearance to comprehend deeper layers of reality.

Being in touch with one's spirituality is to open up new possibilities for relationship with others. It is to connect through that spiritual residue of ourselves that we leave behind us as we go through life by cutting through the baggage of lived experience to the core of one's being. This is what I think happened that night Ruth and I reached out to Iain when he was apparently on his death–bed. I had no reason for doing what I did. It was a reflex response in a situation of trauma which, in a sense, opened me up to certain possibilities despite myself. In fact, if I'd sat down and thought about what to do, I probably wouldn't have done it.

In 1981, a little less than a year after Michelle was born, I received a letter from a woman I just happened to sit beside on a flight from Amsterdam to Toronto. She had seemed vaguely familiar to me but I was unable to place her. The letter read:

Oct. 9, 1981

Dear Professor Turner [X'd out]
    David,
    In 1974–75 I was in hospital (blood clot) and told that I had a 50/50 chance of surviving. I am not telling you this to elicit sympathy!
    It wasn't a great surprise to me, as 3 people had died in my ward by then, and hospitals tend to put like things together.
    Anyway, at the time I had a dream. In this dream a face (I don't *know* what it looked like) and a voice told me that I shouldn't worry, that I would be fine, *not* in the sense that I would live rather than die, but just that everything would be O.K.—and I *believed* it.
    Normally, I don't even remember my dreams, just a few—I'm not presupposing that this was God's voice, by the way—and I am not clairvoyant.
    The point is (I really *don't know* what the point is!) (the *fact*) is that the voice and face was yours. Please, please, *please*, don't think that I'm crazy or foolish (maybe I'm *foolish* sometimes, *very* seldom). I don't expect or want anything from you. I have debated and debated with myself since Wednesday evening as to whether I should tell you.
    But you see it is a little frightening—and who else can I tell? I hope I haven't upset you. It just seems *weird* that I keep running into you—but at the same time, it's sort of like I always knew I would. Why?
    I do *not* have a *vivid* imagination about things of this nature.
    Can you tell me something about this that I don't understand?
    I am tempted to just ignore this whole thing—and you—but *something* stops me and makes me not *want* to.
    Can we talk about this? I will be back in the city on Monday afternoon and evening—can you phone me at . . . .

[signed]

P.S. Now the big question is, Should I send this to you at all?

Probably not. I still wasn't sure just what had happened to me on the train after Michelle was born, and I couldn't see how I could possibly have reached her, let alone reassured her. I was sceptical to say the least—but also somewhat intrigued.

I met her, insisting it be in a public place, and she repeated her story. She said that it was meeting on the 'plane that triggered her "recollection" and that thereafter she'd seen me a number of times on the streets of Toronto. I cross–examined her, questioning every detail. Was she sure it was me? Wasn't her memory playing tricks on her? And why me? I didn't have any abilities like that. She finally left in exasperation. I saw her only once again. She had enrolled in a rather large course I taught at the University but then dropped the class once she realised I knew she was there.

Here was someone saying I had helped her in a profoundly spiritual way—albeit at the time in a way that I did not understand—and I had turned my back on her. Why? For fear that she was wrong, or for fear that she was right?

There is apparently much more to spiritual connectedness than I have as yet realised myself. I was somehow connected to this woman in need without, it appears, any prior association. By the same token, something deeply profound connected me to those swallows in the barn at Notre Dame du Calvaire as well as connected Ellen to Iain and Bryan. Then there was the fortune–teller in Singapore and on the beach in Bali. Perhaps spiritual connections can be made without prior physical association by a simple act of "opening oneself up" and letting the stuff of "nonexistence" flow where it will—to where it is needed. Who knows what untapped well of relational potential lies beneath the surface of human (and nonhuman) nature?

*   *   *   *

In the spring of 1999 I took a step back to the Perth area where most of my spiritual stuff resides. I purchased a cottage on Dalhousie Lake near McDonalds Corners where my parents used to take us during the summers. This rugged country which the locals call the Highland Line was first settled in the 1820s by, as the name implies, dispossessed Scottish Highlanders. A continuity of them remains. Many of them were schoolmates of mine at Perth and District Collegiate Institute—Duncans, Gemmils, Thompsons, Drysdales. Somehow it seems appropriate to start a new life in an old place where the people you know understand you and accept you, flaws and all. I'd like to think that it was being brought up and living here that had something significant to do with my coming to an understanding of the Australians and to where I have now arrived at in my life.

These were people drawn together by the circumstances of their dispossession in the Old Country and by the unforgiving nature of the lands—the rock farms—they were allotted here. From what I know of their history, they certainly helped each other out, person to person, lot to lot, concession to concession, township to township, vocation to vocation. They respected each other's differences as Scottish, Irish, or English—as Catholics or various denominations of Protestantism—as farmers, artisans, or shopkeepers—and used these differences as a means of being mutually accommodating. Here people found a place—were found a place—and the place has always kept a continuity of its people (including its original Native Peoples—the Reeve or Mayor of the Township, Larry McDermott, for instance, is Algonquin).

May 10, 2000: I woke up early this morning and for no apparent reason decided to take my didjeridu down to the dock and play out into the water. It was the first time I'd done this since the ice went out from the lake. So I sat down and began to play a tune I learned from the Aborigines which follows the mouth sound *degul degul, degul degul*, and so on. I played no more than a few bars when I heard a splash in front of me and looked up to see an otter swimming in the water just off shore. It circled as I played, barked a few times and dived. I kept on playing. It resurfaced, swam toward me, then circled again, barked and dived. This went on for half–an–hour. I didn't stop playing until Alexa came down from the cottage and as I turned to tell her what was happening I of course stopped playing. When I turned back to resume playing I saw the otter swimming away to the west, turning back from time to time before disappearing below the water.

The "scientific" explanation for all this is that it was just a coincidence. I just happened to be playing when the otter just happened to be fishing in front of the dock. But this wouldn't explain why the otter came and went with the beginning and end of the music or why he stuck around for so long in such close proximity to me. Normally, an animal like this would vanish at the first sight of a human. You see, that's the thing. The scientific explanation not only can't explain everything, it leaves out the really significant bits. It doesn't explain why the otter gravitated around the sound of the instrument, always keeping it in range so long as I played. It doesn't explain how I felt during the experience, the sense of connectedness to the otter.

Then, a few weeks later I took my didjeridu down to the dock to play again—for the first time since my experience with the otter. I guess about five minutes into my *degul degula* theme I heard a sound. No it wasn't the otter, it was a loon. He was to my right, cruising by and calling out softly over the water—*coo coooo, coo coo*. When he came into line with my instrument, he paused, looked my way, and called again, to which I responded with as best an imitation as I could make of his call over and above my drone. He lingered for a while, moving alternately toward and away from my sound, then he continued on, looking back from time to time as the otter had done.

Would it take three times this time to convince me? No. What happened was spiritual. I somehow tapped into another dimension of reality and communicated with another living being.

January 17, 2001: Last night I awoke about 3 a.m. with a feeling of dread all around me. A peculiar thought came to mind: "There's a disturbance in the force," which, of course, is a line from the movie Star Wars. I felt something had happened to someone close to me. I fell asleep again and awoke about 8 o'clock feeling uneasy. When I arrived at my office to check my e-mail there was one from Grant Burgoyne, Nancy Lalara's husband, my old friend Gula's son–in–law on Groote Eylandt. Gula, he said, had taken ill and was now unable to walk. He had to be carried around, and they weren't sure how much longer he would live. I had just missed seeing him on a brief trip to Australia over Christmas, though I had talked to him on the phone. There was a hint of desperation in his voice at the time and I knew he had wanted very much to see me. Gula does have the power to reach me in spirit and I realized that last night he had.

It was only now that I began to realize the significance of "dreaming" in Gula's way of life and in my own. I have said that I do not attach as much significance to dreams as I do to experience outside myself. This is because I had missed the point. What is significant here is not so much the dream or the vision in question and its location in the psyche as the fact that one is asleep. One's normal sensory apparati—including one's thought categories—are no longer functioning. In other words one is just as open to experiences outside the norm, as when one is in a state of pain or suffering. In such a state things may reach one that might not otherwise.

As it happened, and quite unexpectedly, it was just after Christmas that I had a chance to redeem myself with Gula. David Suzuki's "Sacred Balance" project for the Canadian Broadcasting Corporation (C.B.C.) asked me to take them to the Aboriginal people with whom I worked to film a segment for their programme. So in July, with Alexa, I returned to Darwin and Groote Eylandt and spent time with Gula—perhaps for the last time, as he had suffered a stroke and was hospitalized in Darwin.

February 13, 2002: Today my mother Maud passed away after suffering a stroke on Saturday. She was in her 89th year. Though she could not speak, she could communicate with the squeeze of a hand. She acknowledged everyone as they came to say goodbye before slipping away as Michelle read her an unopened letter we had found on her desk from her sister Irene in England. But before she died, something rather peculiar happened. I was holding her hand when suddenly she raised it up with her own. I thought that she wanted a tissue or something so I lowered it and reached for one. But, again, she took my hand and lifted it, this time pointing upward as she did. I realised that she was seeing something "out there" that she wanted me to see, but I did not. But at that moment I felt that she knew exactly what was happening and where she was going and was at peace. And in and around this moment she accomplished something we had both been wishing for over the past 14 years—reconciliation between Graeme and I.

*   *   *   *

As to the whereabouts of the other people in my tale: Michelle is studying bio–medicine and drama at the University of Guelph and working with children with cancer in the summer. Graeme had been volunteering with Oxfam in Bolivia and he's returned to a job with a computer firm in Ottawa where Ruth still lives. I am back teaching at the University of Toronto and Alexa is happily ensconced at the cottage while I once again commute. Which is where this story began—on the trainline between Toronto and Smiths Falls.

Father Roger is no longer at Notre Dame du Calvaire in New Brunswick but now works at Trinity College at the University of

Toronto. Ketut from Chaumarga in Bali went overseas to Holland to take a hotel management course and returned to Bali to set up eco–tourism. Abdul from Ranikot in Himachal Pradesh did finish his degree at J.N.U. but, as predicted, was unable to find work in government service thereafter. When the Kashmir issue erupted into a small–scale war in 1999, Abdul was harassed by the police as a suspected "terrorist," his people driven from the mountains, and he is now a political refugee living in Paris. His people's fate in India is now even more precarious after the terrible events of September 11th in New York. Sougen Yamakawa of Kokokuji Zen monastery became abbot of Shogen–ji in Gifu and is in demand in Europe and North America as a spokesperson for his faith.

And Iain? I don't know where he is exactly, but from time to time, when I least expect it, I feel him. Last spring, for instance, on a Sunday morning, I was sitting in my front room at the cottage looking out over the lake and listening to the world premiere performance of Philip Glass's "Choral Fifth Symphony" on CBC radio. As I did I slowly became aware of a presence in the room which became so powerful it brought tears to my eyes. I knew it was Iain. The peace and warmth lasted for about an hour and then slowly faded away. He'd made the transition, not from one dimension "here" to another dimension "over there," but to another dimension of "here." At the same time I had made my own transition from grief to acceptance. Now we were both where we should be. I felt joy.

As I mentioned earlier, sceptics who say that a grieving person subconsciously invents experiences such as these in order to make themselves feel better and go on living confuse consequence with cause. The *consequence* of such experiences may be a certain peace of mind, but the *cause* of such experiences is the phenomenon itself.

There are indeed more things in heaven and earth than are dreamt of in our philosophies. It's not that intellectual knowledge, analytical knowledge, is not valuable. Of course it is, as the accomplishments of science attest. It's just that there's a space beyond the intellect, perhaps beyond consciousness, where a different kind of knowledge is revealed—a space beyond the stars and into the "Nothingness" of original creation. Gaze there today and reflect on the full range of possibilities inherent therein we most certainly should.

40. Graeme and Michelle in Darwin

41. Iain at Amagalyuagba, Bickerton Island

LORD OF THE DANCE
(traditional, Shaker)

Figure 2.